The Person

The Person

I, Wisdom
(God in the Time Realm)

Ian Heard

RESOURCE *Publications* • Eugene, Oregon

THE PERSON
I, Wisdom (God in the Time Realm)

Copyright © 2019 Ian Heard. All rights reserved. Except for brief quotations in critical publications or reviews, no part of this book may be reproduced in any manner without prior written permission from the publisher. Write: Permissions, Wipf and Stock Publishers, 199 W. 8th Ave., Suite 3, Eugene, OR 97401.

Resource Publications
An Imprint of Wipf and Stock Publishers
199 W. 8th Ave., Suite 3
Eugene, OR 97401

www.wipfandstock.com

PAPERBACK ISBN: 978-1-7252-5873-0
HARDCOVER ISBN: 978-1-7252-5874-7
EBOOK ISBN: 978-1-7252-5875-4

Manufactured in the U.S.A.   12/17/19

Contents

Introduction | vii
Chapter 1: In the beginning . . . I, Wisdom | 1
Chapter 2: The Un-Wising | 7
Chapter 3: Wisdom in Election | 11
Chapter 4: Wisdom in Covenant | 17
Chapter 5: Wisdom in Ten Words | 23
Chapter 6: Wisdom embedded | 30
Chapter 7: History is Mine | 35
Chapter 8: Wisdom in Correction and Foresight | 37
Chapter 9: A Zenith in shadow form | 40
Chapter 10: The Promise | 45
Chapter 11: Memra and Logos | 48
Chapter 12: Wisdom and Time | 54
Chapter 13: The Denouement | 59
Chapter 14: Man in grey meets Wisdom in White | 62
Chapter 15: Darkness comprehended it not | 66
Chapter 16: Among you! | 69
Chapter 17: Salvation: Wising up! | 75
Chapter 18: The House that Wisdom built | 78
Afterword by Watcher Shaqaad | 84

> Those who are wise shall shine
> Like the brightness of the firmament,
> And those who turn many to righteousness
> Like the stars forever and ever.
>
> —DANIEL 12:3, NKJV

Introduction

I SEE THAT MY book about The People: The sons of God[1] has 'seen the light of day', to use one of your human expressions—and so I now wish to follow it with another. It's about how Yahweh Elohim inserted himself into the warp and weft of his own creation to be the very means by which rescue for those known as benei adam (the sons of men), could be effected.

Yes, I am Shaqaad, the one . . .the Watcher-being, who led you through the extraordinary story of The People—his people. But it's important to see that at no moment through your time journey on Earth has he ever been far from you. Oh no! For, immediately upon your failure to remain joined with him at your beginning, he implemented a plan by which he might woo and win you back to himself.

In seeking to help you see how the Elohim One has, as I said, inserted himself into the warp and weft of creation's fabric and history, I intend to speak in the first person—yes, as though I were he!

My hope is that my readers will not conclude this to be presumptuous on my part—after all, I am but a created being as are you! Rather, as one among those who has always both worshiped and obeyed him, I believe I know his heart well enough to indulge a little presumption in the hope of helping some of you human beings see what you may not as yet, have seen.

Of course, you have the holy scriptures, the sure record by which he has been marvellously revealed and it would never be my

1. 'THE PEOPLE: the sons of God (through the eyes of a Watcher) Wipf and Stock ISBN 978-1-5326-4828-1

Introduction

intention to detract from, nor add to, their authority and validity. Insofar as written words are concerned, in them alone is life; the Life of Yahweh Elohim himself, so you must go first to them and only ever to the writings of others inasmuch as they shed light on or point to, those inspired words.

I am doing as one of the inspired authors within that holy writ has done, speaking in the first person, as though an aspect of the Elohim One's glorious nature and character. Hear me as I attempt to follow the great Shalomoh's[2] example in this. I do so only because it delights me, Shaqaad, to speak of my Lord and Sovereign and to bring honour to him. I shall do my best . . .

Yours in Yahweh's everlasting thrall,
WATCHER SHAQAAD

---

2. Solomon in Proverbs

CHAPTER 1

In the beginning...I, Wisdom

*I **wisdom**...was beside Him as a master craftsman...*
—PROVERBS 8:12–30, NJKV

*...He has established the world by His **wisdom**, and stretched out the heaven by His understanding*
—JEREMIAH 51:15, NKJV

*To Him who by **wisdom** made the heavens*
—PSALM 136:4–5, NKJV

I AM WISDOM. I am known also by other names as you will see as we proceed. I was there when your realm and world were spoken into reality. In fact, it was *my* voice that spoke! When I say 'into reality', I mean into a construct that has, to you who inhabit it, the appearance of reality...of substance. Although having the appearance of permanence, it is however, but transient and fleeting. It will be shown (eventually) as not being of the eternal kind of reality in which I exist (and of which I desire all to become part). At the end it will be shown, in fact, to be expendable—and will be burned up.[1] The created cosmos in which you exist is a world of particles:

---

1. See, for example 2 Peter 3:10

that is, it was made of what you call matter, being particulate and atomic in form. The particles range from huge and vast like your Sun and other stars, down to sizes which are only now being discovered in your day and time, but even so, the large objects (say like, prunes, planets and stars) are made also of infinitesimal particles. Indeed, what you call the 'quantum' realm is giving your physicists a glimpse into the boundary between the world you occupy, and mine! And, as you have found, the rules that govern the very large (by which I mean planets or tennis balls or even grains of sand) are not the same as those that apply at the quantum level. The realm that I occupy, you may be surprised to learn, is not a particle world at all. No . . .it is the realm of spirit—a different realm and platform entirely! Mind you, you also are actually of my realm, but in your case, Yahweh Elohim has housed your spirit within a material or physical 'carriage' for your journey in time. He always intended you to have eternality. That's why he created you as a spirit being—a non-particulate being, though housed within a material, particulate body.

Had your first parents kept on engaging with me as I desired, things for you would have been altogether different. As it is, they failed and in so doing condemned your realm to severe limitations—oh, you can never know how severe! However, it was out of unimaginable love that you were created and it is from that same inexhaustible love that he, Yahweh Elohim, is redeeming a now spoiled creation.

There is to be a new one, yes, a new creation and his desire is that you be part of it. Yes, you who read and heed! In fact, you are the beginning of this new creation . . .if you will allow him to re-create *you*.

Let me tell you about myself. To you who read (those beings called human, created to be analogous to the great Yahweh Elohim) . . .he has shown forth me as the 'first' (by which he really means the foundational platform) of his creative activity within your realm.[2]

---

2. Proverbs 8:22 where the Hebrew means something like, 'he constituted and established me as the foundation (or head or chief) of the creation journey

In the beginning . . . I, Wisdom

Let me explain: you humans say that you like to understand where another person is 'coming from' and by this you mean that you want to comprehend the platform within them from which their worldview, arises. So, you are inclined to say when you don't understand someone, "I don't know where she's coming from."

You know that there is such a 'platform' from which people function and that from that platform they too create things—things which inevitably bear in some way, their 'likeness and image.' You are able therefore to recognize what they produce, as uniquely theirs. Take some of your great artists or composers, for example: their work is usually distinctive so that you are able to say, "that is Chopin" or, "that is the work of Monet." When you begin to know another human well, you can, to a certain extent, predict their verbal or other responses to situations and stimuli. This is when it can be said that you truly know someone.

In the case of Yahweh Elohim, the platform from which he expressed himself in his creation—that is, where he was 'coming from' was me—and I was best described as . . . Wisdom![3] (And, before someone says, "no . . . but surely the platform was love," allow me time to explain). It is, in its entirety, a work that displays foremost, his Wisdom. He desired his all-wise-ness to be recognized as the platform upon which it all stood—Wisdom that would cause you to fall down in undone wonder! For it is written into every particle of the creation in which you participate! Scientists of your day are discovering the phenomenon of your own constitution, so long hidden, in what is now called DNA. (It's a shame so many of you choose deliberately to believe that your own wisdom matches his and that it's only a matter of time before it is all understood and therefore, mastered. I can assure you; it will never be). I see that one of your own has well-described him as the Alone-Wise.[4] Yes, the Elohim One is Wisdom's source and his Wisdom is manifest

OR' YAHWEH had ordained me as the head of his works.' The word translated 'beginning' here is RESHITH from ROSH meaning head or chief.

3. Hebrew CHOCKMAH—in human terms, the ability to always choose correctly for best outcome.

4. Paul in Romans 16:27

The Person

throughout his mysterious three-in-one personhood as you will see as I share more with you.

I, Wisdom am that Platform from which both your visible and invisible world sprang; and I was employed as the word and the voice speaking your time and space realm into being. Then, within it, a created order of beings with grand and (to you) only partially fathomable purpose. But he has shown you enough, by various and many means, to enable you to grasp his extraordinary desire for *you*—the one and only creature in his image! As one of your own has so well expressed it—

'Oh, the depth of the riches both of the wisdom and knowledge of God! How unsearchable are His judgments and His ways past finding out! "For who has known the mind of the Lord? Or who has become His counselor?" Or who has first given to Him and it shall be repaid to him? For of Him and through Him and to Him are all things, to whom be glory forever. Amen."[5]

And so it was expressed also in the Writings, 'Yahweh constituted *me* as the head of his works'[6] and so it was both from me and upon me, that your earth—and the entire created fabric of which you occupy such a tiny part—was founded! It is a work of astounding Wisdom.

Now of course, when the Elohim One said, "let us make man" the *motive* behind that "let us," was love; love of a kind that desired an object, albeit living within a different realm yet having similar capacity to both give and receive, love! Other created beings were not of the extraordinary autonomy and 'likeness' with which you are endowed. And that is why he uniquely put into you an 'I-am-ness' just like his! You are a work motivated by the love of his 'begetting' heart (and is of course why you also have the desire to beget) and a manifestation of all-wise-ness quite beyond human comprehension—but not beyond human adoration and worship.

So, you see, Love was *the motive*; and Wisdom, *the means*.

The Elohim, Creator, the great Yahweh having all *knowledge*, chose to create by *wisdom*; for wisdom is but knowledge employed

---

5. Paul in Romans 11:33–36
6. Proverbs 8:22 see Footnote 2.

In the beginning . . . I, Wisdom

to greatest fruitfulness. Wisdom acts always with the best outcome in view. In your own case, a work arising from your knowledge alone is in danger of becoming a vanity. Humans make some things because of knowledge, but do not always exhibit wisdom in both the making and the using of them: nor is the motive always self-giving love. Sometimes the foundation and reason for existence of things manufactured is 'because we can' or, 'because it will enhance my recognition' but these are not necessarily wise reasons. All that the Elohim One has made in and through me, expresses purpose and the desire for perfect product.

As well as wisdom, the works also declare his holiness, majesty, limitlessness and character. You know immediately what he is like (and who he is) simply by looking at his work! Unless, of course you are among those who prefer to pretend that what they see arose mysteriously of its own volition and 'desire', un-made, and yet existing—without cause—and void of purpose! That some choose to exercise a belief in that direction is, of course a Creator-given and permitted prerogative; yet it is also (as you may imagine) a matter of great pain to him just as it would be to you if others credited your work as having a different origin. That you humans are free and therefore able, to make that choice, is perhaps one of the most extraordinary expressions of his wisdom—and of his desire to have a creature as analogous to himself as possible—inhabiting the created time-realm.

I, Wisdom know that his (shall I now say 'our'?) desire was and is, a creature as free and yet as responsible, as our self. But for the creature to be like that, requires my presence—maintained within—by choice!

When knowledge is chosen above wisdom (as your first parents chose), clearly wisdom is relegated and therefore diminished. This is why you humans must be so careful in your choices. The temptation and pretense of Knowledge is that by it you will eventually achieve mastery over everything. That is un-wise; it is in fact, a blasphemy because all that is lasting (that is, eternal) and in accord with our purpose, is a work of wisdom first. This is exactly why in our words to you we have so often said that, 'the fear of

The Person

Yahweh is the *beginning* of wisdom, and to *know* the Holy One is understanding."[7] Wisdom may employ knowledge, but only insofar as it assists in the creation of that which is like its Origin; what is wholly good and works to fulfill his purpose and design. And have I not been trying to teach you throughout your time journey that your Destiny is beyond and above Time and earth-bound-ness? It is a tragic thing that many of your greatest minds have made the mistake of believing that true-self and true-heart—and even immortality—can be discovered at the tree of Knowledge when I have made it clear that anything of eternal worth must have its foundation in wisdom; in Me. With me is the Tree of Life!

It is I who speak now to show that not only was I there at your beginning—that you, the greatest of his creative works, are a product of Wisdom—but also that I have been travelling the span of your time with you, always offering evidence for those with eyes to see and ears to hear . . .

> **Wisdom** *calls aloud outside; She raises her voice in the open squares. She cries out in the chief concourses, At the openings of the gates in the city She speaks her words:*
> *"How long, you simple ones, will you love naïveté?"*[8]

---

7. See Proverbs 9:10, Psalm 111:10 and Job 28:28
8. Proverbs 1:20–22a

CHAPTER 2

The Un-Wising

PART OF CREATOR'S PLEASURE in his work was the diffusion of our essence into you, his new order of beings. The first of you, 'Dam, became a living and sentient being when (and because) Elohim 'breathed' life from himself into him! What he breathed was an 'I am' self-identity, reflecting his I AM! Without that there was, and is, no being; no selfhood. He was imparting his likeness to you; his similitude! He said, "let us make man as an image of us, resembling us; let them have dominion over . . .all the earth . . ."[1] You became a creature analogous to us, within the created time and particle realm. We see that clever, though fallen ones of your kind and in every age, try desperately to avoid or to ignore this self-evident and inescapable truth. (I say inescapable, because a day comes when my view *will*, too late, become that of every liar and deny-er!)

Can you see that you were created as regents?[2] And you were given, as part of making you analogous, wisdom and authority for your regency. Dominion over a realm created of Wisdom implies and demands wisdom. Rulership was a trust from him providing opportunity for wisdom to be exercised—as an extension of his. Yes, I, Wisdom was to continue to dance with you in the luxury of co-creation and stewardship to bring your realm into its discovery of unhindered bounty. Wisdom to rule was breathed into you, yet

---

1. Genesis 1:26
2. A regent is defined as a person appointed to administer a state.

it remained yours to keep just as any gift is kept; by choice. That is why we had to allow the possibility for you to act independently.

Greater trust, expansion and productivity—indeed, co-creativity, was made contingent upon you exercising your will to keep me as the 'platform' from which you also were 'coming'. The opportunity therefore, to become 'un-wise'—to 'un-wise' yourself, did exist. The Gift could actually be rejected...and was! The opportunity to exchange it for something less, which was made to *appear* more desirable, was offered by the first of the unwise. Indeed, by that master of un-wisdom—the one who, although once of lofty and magnificent glory, coveted the glory of the Elohim One and had thereby suffered immediate and automatic expulsion from our presence. It is not possible for anything impure to abide here, such is the Presence of the Holy! I speak of great mystery and truths not yet disclosed to your kind. It is part of the trust to which he calls you, just as he called the first of your kind. Do not fail as they did.

The Choice

*'Does not **wisdom** cry out? She takes her stand . . .*
where the paths meet . . .

My voice is to the sons of men (benei adam)[3]

"O, you naïve ones . . . be of an understanding heart"[4]

My voice was there to be heard. The Elohim walked with you in that garden as your record says. We always ensured that our voice was present to hear so that you could be constantly choosing...us. We made the choice clear then, as we continue to do in your day. At the crossroads, 'where the paths meet'; the choice to stay with us, to keep the gift and therefore, its fruit.

---

3. See this author's book 'THE PEOPLE, The Sons of God (through the eyes of a Watcher)' which contrasts the sons of men (benei adam) with the sons of God (benei Elohim) throughout the Bible.

4. From Proverbs 8:1–5 NJKV emphasis added

The Un-Wising

That choice always results in good and abounding fruit. It was the choice in Gan Edhen,[5] where you valued knowledge above wisdom for life and productivity; you were deceived by the lie that knowledge or intelligence[6] would make you like Elohim, and by the inference that he was withholding something from you. Do you now see what a deception that was? You were being offered something that was in fact, already yours and which you simply needed to appreciate by daily choosing! It was not *knowledge* that would make you like him—you were already like him. You *were* analogous, possessing wisdom—and I was present to be taken continually from the Tree of Life; but in grasping for knowledge you forfeited wisdom. This saddened the great heart of Elohim; saddened us. I was there; my voice was pleading. You could have been continually filled with me, Wisdom, and your path would have been so different—abounding with productivity and without the evils of pain and struggle and death. Do you see now what grasping after a deceit, did? You allowed yourself to be robbed; it was, sadly, the naïve choice, leading you away from your destined fruitfulness in the Garden.

The same offer is of course, still being made in your day, leading many to exalt knowledge over wisdom, as though intelligence will manufacture the answers for every human need. But knowledge without wisdom is a vanity, for wisdom is the righteous search for, and implementation of, knowledge. It is knowledge put to its best, most beneficial purpose. And herein lies the ongoing choice, given daily to all people. I cry out continually— 'my voice is to the sons of men.' I stand at every crossroad of life and circumstance— 'where the paths meet' and I call, "choose me!"

It's not that your realm or time is devoid entirely of wisdom. Oh no . . .there are many vestiges of it and there are some who, although they do not yet incline their hearts to Yahweh, nonetheless,

---

5. Garden of Eden

6. Eve understood the tempter to be offering something that would make her clever; the Hebrew SAKAL means intelligence or cleverness. The trick was to cause her to believe that God had withheld something from them that should be theirs.

The Person

do choose wisdom. What they have perhaps not seen is that when they do, they are nearer to us than they would like to admit. The two trees still stand and beckon. I am within one, the one to be chosen first . . .the One called Life. When you *choose* to eat of me and live by my fruit, you'll be surprised how knowledge—knowledge of the holy, knowledge of me and my ways and how to walk in them—follows!

I will continue to beckon and to make it possible to find me and live in my offer of Life. This is the real knowledge. It is important to understand, as has been written by wise men in your annals about our work among you, that knowledge is for the mind, whilst wisdom is for the heart; and it is the heart that is the seat of motive and action—

> *When wisdom enters your heart,*
> *And knowledge is pleasant to your soul,*
> *Discretion will preserve you;*
> *Understanding will keep you,*
> *To deliver you from the way of evil,*
> *From the man who speaks perverse things*[7]

In your day, humans, in grasping (so often competitively) for knowledge, have missed wisdom for life. It has been truly said by one of the great ones that we gave you along the way—that man Daniʼel— that as earth time winds down, 'many will run back and forth and *knowledge* will multiply.'[8] It is a sign and it will be seen (by the few) that even as knowledge multiplies exponentially, and many applaud the wonders, there is also a corresponding and exponential loss, of wisdom.

I, Wisdom, still raise my voice in the squares, in the gates and where the paths meet. Yes, I may be heard. But it requires a certain kind of listening, because loud, very loud, are the voices raised with the intention of preventing you from heeding! It is my hope that as we continue this journey together, you will see how.

---

7. Proverbs 2:10–12
8. Daniel 12:4 where 'knowledge' is the Hebrew word YADA.

CHAPTER 3

Wisdom in Election

> *Oh, the depth of the riches both of the **wisdom** and knowledge of God! How unsearchable are His judgments and His ways past finding out! "For who has known the mind of the Lord? Or who has become His counselor? Or who has first given to Him and it shall be repaid to him?" For of Him and through Him and to Him are all things, to whom be glory forever. Amen.*
>
> —ROMANS 11:33–36, NKJV

> *For since, in the **wisdom** of God, the world through (its) **wisdom** did not know God, it pleased God through the foolishness of the message preached to save those who believe.*
>
> —1 CORINTHIANS 1:21, NKJV

TO YOU, HISTORY—THE UNFOLDING of time—appears to be made up of a series of events or occurrences, some of which seem somewhat predictable, whilst others are totally random. This is a fact with which philosophers of every one of your ages has wrestled. I understand that it is difficult for earthbound creatures to have a large enough perspective to see what I see. You cannot get back far enough to see the whole thing as I am able. And that is exactly why the Father calls for trust. He's the One with the Big picture! Yes, to many it seems like a big call—there is so much distress, trauma, difficulty and dilemma in your world. But once you see why—that it is because it is a spoiled vestige of its created self, you are just beginning the journey along the track whose destination is surrender—to him; the point at which you will be, at last, prepared to trust. Yes, it *is* a big ask, especially as around you there is a world almost full of un-surrender and un-trust. But, it is important to know that he would not ask it of you if it were not possible—and more simply possible than you think!

Actually, many of you already have a kind of trust; it's just in things other than him—things which can only eventually and ultimately prove untrustworthy! For some of you have a kind of trust that Science (Knowledge) will, in the end, meet every human need. Others trust money and accumulations; and yet others, trust that they are, on average, as 'good' as most others. That if there is, perchance, a being or system to whom we eventually answer—he, she or it will find them somewhere in the middle of what you call the bell-curve of what's acceptable for whatever is to come later. Lots of people-groups in your past trusted, and even today trust ancestors to help them on their journey into the afterlife. The common human discovery however, is that trust in any or even all of these things never provides any true comfort or indeed, any feedback. True, money may provide a sense of comfort and temporary security—as may a bottle of whiskey; but of course, the bottle will empty and riches can be lost overnight or ill-health or death may remove you from them at any moment. The future is your killer! Its fickle-ness or even its false promises may spoil joy at any moment. Elation can become extreme disappointment or even despair, overnight.

Something better is needed . . . and is offered. I, Wisdom will come to that . . .

Some of those who put their trust in Knowledge (or Science as it is called in your day) believe that what is visible (or deduced from what is visible), is all there is—and that it all ultimately has no meaning unless you can, through your own cleverness, discover or manufacture one. It all 'occurred' and came into being through blind, meaningless chance and will go on being governed by blind, meaningless chance! The only meaning to be extracted from this

Wisdom in Election

belief system (it's no comfort) is that somehow, by the same meaningless process by which it came into being you will 'evolve' into something improved (whatever that means!). If there is trust or belief at all, it is that you are, by knowledge and cleverness, making your way to eventual mastery over creation's 'problems'; war, famine, greed, corruption, disease or even ageing!

And now we are getting close to the reason he has given you creatures of time, a beautiful record; one that takes you from beginning to end and is full of meaning and purpose and hope for any whose ears and eyes will open and whose heart is ready. It requires a willingness to receive, to believe and to trust. That is the leap—or so it appears; but it's actually a step only, and one in which there hides a surprise. For it will be found that he, indeed we, meet you at that first voluntary step, with wide-open arms—to embrace you, welcome you—and even carry you to help you come 'home'!

Taste and Sight

Do you now know why I stand at every crossroad, calling? Once you become willing to turn your head, you will wonder why you had refused to hear and see and to act, earlier. For it is the answer hidden almost in plain sight, like something in your peripheral vision, of which you are just conscious. It requires a certain kind of response from the creature; a deliberate turning of the head; a resolve to act, to 'taste and *see*' as one of you own has so wisely written.[1] It had been in Gan Edhen that Lucifer held out a false prospect of opened eyes, new sight—and cleverness[2]—for a taste of the forbidden tree; but I was not to be found there. Ironically, his offer also was, 'taste and *see*.' In that garden, two particular kinds of 'seeing' resulted from tasting; one kind of sight came from tasting

---

1. Psalm 34:8 'Oh *taste* and *see* that the LORD is good; blessed is the one who *trusts* in him' *emphasis* added.

2. In Genesis 3:5 and 6 the serpent said "you will be like God, knowing good and evil" and Eve understood this as meaning it was "desirable to make one *intelligent*." The Hebrew word is SAKAL, is like, but not the same as, wisdom.

The Person

the tree of Life, and an altogether different kind from the tree of Knowledge. Eyes *were* opened at the tasting of that tree, but you did not enjoy what was revealed and its consequences were grave.

The getting of wisdom begins, counter-intuitively, in the (at first alien) direction away from self-trust, self-sufficiency and even self-righteousness, toward willingness to become child-like; a learner and a listener—to me, Wisdom. Wisdom from above.[3] For the earth and all that is of it, yes, even all knowledge, will fail you. It is destined for an end, a destruction, whereas my realm is eternal and what I have to say, if acted upon, will usher you into its dynamic, both now and afterwards.

The record I earlier spoke of is that of my work through your time history to try to bring you the big view, the view of him who created both it and you, for great and everlasting purpose.

It is I, Wisdom who has spoken in that record. You must go to it. If necessary, you must ask for help in understanding it. That is why I have given you in your day, a presence in the earth, my proxy in both Spirit and Body; and within that Body I have given a panoply of provision for receiving wisdom; they are called apostles, prophets, evangelists, pastors and teachers.[4]

But I must return to my direction, for the view—the perspective and Wisdom from my realm— has not only been revealed in creation but then in our election and setting apart of a people (who became known as The People).[5] Their role was to portray, to make evident within a world gone wrong, myself—Wisdom,[6] in Yahweh's grace-filled plan. It is true that it's a mystery that he chose to reveal me through a people, yet that is the nature of his

---

3. See James 3:17 'But the wisdom that is from above is first pure, then peaceable, gentle, willing to yield, full of mercy and good fruits, without partiality and without hypocrisy.'

4. Ephesians 4:11ff. All these are gifts to the Church for every age.

5. See this author's book 'THE PEOPLE: the sons of God (through the eyes of a Watcher)' Wipf and Stock ISBN:978-1-5326-4828-1 (Paperback) or 978-1-5326-4830-4 (EBOOK)

6. Deuteronomy 4:6 ' . . .for this will show your *wisdom* in the sight of the peoples . . .who will hear and say "surely this great nation is a *wise* and understanding people"'

Wisdom in Election

love and the hope that he continually places in those who choose him. The People were, well . . .people; flawed, often self-centered, even rebellious and intransigent! And yet, and yet . . .we brought our purpose to pass through them—which should give all of your humankind, hope! For he has shown himself repeatedly as a Redeemer; of flawed people—and of purpose—and even of time! A Redeemer. Yes, it is so! (Taste and see!).

I want you to see that I was there at the beginning of the choosing of that people. As you've seen, one of your writers said of me, 'does not Wisdom cry out? . . .she takes her stand on the top of the high hill, beside the way, where the paths meet . . .to you, O men, I call, and my voice is to the sons of men[7] (benei adam).'"[8]

A man at the crossroads

There was a particular man who stood where paths met, and whom I was instructed to call. He was at Charan where his father Terah and family had halted on a journey which Yahweh would have them pursue but where the father had begun to worship strange gods.[9]

Now, Charan was a significant place for the son, whose name was Avram. Avram had experienced my call some time before when the family was still living in Naharayim (or Mesopotamia as the reader will know it).[10] But now they had journeyed to this place, Charan, whose name in your language means Crossroads—where the paths meet.[11] It is at such places that I am often instructed to make my call heard, as I was on this occasion. It was I, Wisdom calling this man to whom Father had directed me at this moment along the line you call time! Calling him to leave the folly of old

---

7. Proverbs 8:1–4
8. See 'The People' as per footnote 5 above.
9. Joshua 24:2, 14
10. In Acts 7:2–3 Stephen said that Abraham was called whilst in Mesopotamia, *before* he dwelt in Haran (Charan).
11. The Hebrew Charan or Haran means Crossroads. See http://bibleapps.com/hebrew/2771a.htm

dependencies and to come to the Wisdom of dependence on Yahweh Elohim. And this man, later to be called Ivrahim,[12] rose to the challenge! He chose the way of wisdom. He chose me—and in so doing became an example for the ages.

This was our sovereign election call. The level to which those of Naharayim had sunk in moving away from the trust of which I speak, was appalling. It was time for Yahweh to step in (once again) with a new start. And he chose the man, Avram—and I, Wisdom, was involved in that call—even before he arrived in Charan. This man was to become Father to a new people, The People, who would represent Yahweh and his wisdom to the world!

Yahweh Elohim is the God of new beginnings. It is because of the corruption within creation and, ever-so-sadly, within the creature formed as a spirit-being in his likeness, that these new beginnings are required. You see, the corruption is like yeast. Its work is difficult to confine or contain. There is a nadir or low point at which Yahweh must, to use one of your own expressions, 'draw a line in the sand.' That point is, when the sons of men (the benei adam) practice the sacrifice of their own children, and I see that in the days of you who read, this deception is again overtaking you; and I, Wisdom must shout, 'Beware!'[13]

---

12. Ivrahim (or Abraham as we know him), means 'Father of many nations.'

13. In the form of child abortion. Abortions worldwide now (2019) exceed 40,000,000 per annum according to the World Health Organisation.

CHAPTER 4

Wisdom in Covenant

DEAR READER, I WANT to introduce you to the way the Elohim One works in his masterplan to restore our entire creation from its state of alienation and lostness, to its intended glory. For glorious it was; and glorious it will be again!

To assist you I will further explain about this man who proved himself to be a true friend of Yahweh Elohim[1]—this man Avram whose name was changed to Ivrahim and who became an exemplar of the relationship Yahweh wishes to have with each of you. My reason for bringing you in on the essence of my discourse with him below is to help you see the idea and importance of what your scriptures call, Covenant. The unfolding discourse with our friend went along these lines . . .

Ivrahim: "O great Wisdom of Yahweh. You were one of the Three who visited me when I was camped by the great terebinth trees near Mamre Brook.[2] I have never forgotten. I knew then who you were . . .I had been conscious of your nearness many times— and of your favor. One of those occasions was shortly after my encounter with the one, Malkhi-Tzedek of Salem—at HaMakom, The Place.[3] You had spoken into my inmost heart that day and I knew it to be the voice of Wisdom that came not from within me! You gave me a promise that was beyond my wildest imagining . . .

1. See James 2:23
2. See Genesis 18
3. See this author's book 'THE PLACE HaMakom; where Jerusalem's Temples stood.'

I, Wisdom: "Ah, and what occurred then was of the very greatest significance. It is the essence of what I desire my readers to see.

Ivrahim: "you mean when Yahweh had me go outside the tent and try to count the stars?"

I, Wisdom: "Yes, I want to hear about it in your own words."

Ivrahim: "Well, it was a most numinous and awesome thing . . .there was I under a million stars which seemed like holes of light in a tent much vaster than mine; it was as though they were somehow awaiting the outcome of something of great portent. You had spoken into my heart the promise of my very own son! I had lamented that it looked as though Elyezer my steward, would be my heir—and right then, into my inmost heart, you communicated in an undeniable way that an heir would come from my own body and, what's more, that my descendants would be as those stars I could not count! And then . . .and then, you had me bring a heifer and a goat and a ram, a turtledove and a young pigeon, all of which except the birds, I was to cut in two and lay on the ground opposite each other . . .

I, Wisdom: "Aha—did you have then an inkling of what this meant?"

Ivrahim: "I recognized that you wanted to make—or 'cut' as we say— an agreement with me. I had had enough experience by now of what occurs in our human agreements and how we seal them as binding. And I had also my very personal experiences of your providence and presence to be expectant. I just did it . . .but it had made a long day, preparing the three-year-old heifer and goat and ram, not to mention the birds and then trying to keep the ravenous vultures from them until darkness came. I was exhausted . . .

I, Wisdom: "Can we pause there? Can you see any significance in those vultures trying to steal what you had prepared?"

Ivrahim: "They were doing what vultures do; how often have I seen it? But it did occur to me that since you were behind this—whatever it was—that dark forces may be trying to prevent it. But I succeeded in keeping them off because I knew something was afoot! And of course, now I know I was right to do so."

WISDOM IN COVENANT

I, Wisdom: "Indeed you were. Whenever we are taking one of you somewhere not traversed before—taking you into a new place or a new level of dependence on us, there are indeed dark forces bent on robbing the flow of life that is to come from the obedience. So, please continue...exhausted from your efforts you fell into deep sleep right there under that blazing canopy—and experienced within what you had seen occur with those huge, screeching, ravenous birds. You sensed that it had deep significance in the spiritual realm and this is one of the reasons you will be known as 'the friend of Yahweh.' You are to exemplify that heart; it is the heart we are looking for in all. Indeed, it is possible for all, even though dark powers may try to rob and prevent. But, continue please."

Ivrahim: "I awoke to the most extraordinary sight: for a smoking fire-carrying vessel together with a lit firebrand appeared passing between those pieces—and then Yahweh said that he was making a special kind of agreement with me...with *me!* It is what we call a berith and it is a promise, sealed in this case with the lifeblood of animals on my part, and on yours, with a symbol of your presence to seal the compact."

I, Wisdom: "So Ivrahim, can you explain what you understood by this 'berith?'"

Ivrahim: "Indeed, I understood it to be a promise...an unconditional promise from you to me, based entirely on sovereign grace and your ability to perform what I cannot."

I, Wisdom: "Aha, you have it! For that is, and must always be, the basis of our work with you and with all who follow and you who read; our work of redemption. And not just in the matter of an heir for you. You are seeing a larger picture also, for the meaning is that all the sons of men are incapable of self-redemption because that which has become unsound cannot make itself again sound. What means would it employ to do so? That which cannot bear fruit on its own as you dear Ivrahim have found, must cooperate with the one who can. You may think it to be a one-sided affair—and yes, it is; for it is of the same nature as our creation of you; it was not of you! In that act, you played no role; you exist only by our volition, plan, and of course, the desire of love.

And so in this; you may cooperate with us in it . . .and you must, if you are to be made sound again. But it is of us: let that be clear and beyond any misinterpretation or misunderstanding! If that is not understood you will spend fruitless time and energy in attempts to do it yourself or to make for yourself a role in it that you can never have. Acceptance and joyful cooperation is your part! That, is the getting of wisdom!

"Ivrahim, your part here was cooperating in giving and yielding up and making ready the heifer and the goat and ram . . .and the birds. Yielding is your cooperation with me. I do the rest—and then it becomes fact! And dear Ivrahim, let it be seen that our requirement for a heifer, a ram and a goat and turtle dove and a pigeon signify to all who come from you and for all time, that no-one is excluded. Our grace is for all . . .and is experienced in the yielding."

Ivrahim: "O Lord, I see it; and I desire that in my yielded life there be an example for all."

I, Wisdom: "It shall be so."

Of course, I reminded Ivrahim also of his fortuitous encounter with the mysterious priest Malchi-Tzedek who, as was seen later, and in hindsight, was a sign and 'type' of my arrival in flesh among you. That one signified a permanent and lasting priesthood that stood above the temporary one which was soon to be launched.

I have told you about faith-filled Ivrahim because he typifies the basis upon which your relationship with us is to function. You are to trust. There is no other way.

From narrow to wide

Many wonder at our election of a single human through whom to begin the unfolding of large purpose, but it is our way. For we know the human heart and have found it best to begin with a clear and indubitable call on one person from whom we can work in an outward direction as the ripples from a pebble dropped in a pond begin from a point, and affect the whole body of water.

Our principle is like that of just a small piece of leaven working within the massive lump of dough until the whole is leavened! And so, we chose and called a man who saw and heard and 'got' where we were coming from—and whom we could call 'friend.' That one man became the exemplar for all—yes, *all* the nations and peoples—because of his obedience. And once we had his heart and his trust (for he proved to us that he trusted totally that we would cause everything to work to our plan as well as to his great benefit) we knew that hope was born once again within mankind. And, we were able to keep demonstrating, yes, despite his human-ness, that our choice or election is definite, clear and best. For example, having promised Ivrahim a son through whom our promise would unfold—and since he could see no possibility because of Sarai's age—he and Sarai went ahead and used Hagar, Sarai's maidservant as a surrogate mother.

But no! The son born this way was not the son of *our* promise! Not the one *we* had in mind! And so we had to show them both a better way, the way they had deemed impossible. Yes, the greatly aged Sarai gave birth to Yitzchak so that our plan could proceed.

Again, and later, we had to demonstrate that it is Yahweh Elohim's plan which is in train, not man's! For in similar demonstration, when Yitzchak's sons were to be born, we promised Yitzchak and Ribqueh that of the twins about to be born, the older would serve the younger! Yes, against all human custom or tradition, *we* would unfold the plan in our own particular way. And so it was, as you know from the annals, that Esav's right of birth as firstborn was purloined by Yaakov! It is a long story, but one in which we kept showing that *we* were in charge of the unfolding!

From wide to narrow

The people arising from Ivrahim and Yitzchak became a great people...until once more they became constrained through their own folly and we had to choose another individual through whom to continue our great plan. Yes, his name was Moshe; human, weak, willful—but our chosen one; specifically chosen for our people's deliverance. The pebble for the new pond.

You will see that we kept on doing this along your timeline, your history; this narrowing down to a person whose influence under ours spread throughout our called people—The People. A part of the reason for this was because of the dilution of Truth the further in time it is removed from its source, just as the pond ripples diminish with time and distance. And they also become corrupted by ripples from other sources. The second part of the reason is that we desired always to be 'typifying' and pointing forward to a full and final answer: One in whom the promise to Ivrahim—and all the promises we made thereafter, came to fulfilment! Not a pebble, but One known as 'The Rock.'

CHAPTER 5

Wisdom in Ten Words

Lostness and Found-ness

LOSTNESS IS A FRIGHTENING thing. Some will have childhood memories of becoming separated from parents in a crowded place. Until that moment of awareness of separation arrives, all is well: in that instant, dread engulfs. I, Wisdom have seen it—and indeed on more than one such occasion, intervened. I have felt that which was in a child's being at that moment and discerned it as abject helplessness and terror. All was well until that one, waking instant. It is also true that there are children in your world who grow up in a state of separation; street orphans and the abandoned who learn all kinds of pernicious ways to keep themselves alive and surviving. They have become inured to their lostness; do not understand that they are lost because lostness is the only life they have experienced. They have no real desire to be 'found' because they have never experienced 'found-ness'; never experienced lovingkindness, provision and care from another.

Now in the world you inhabit, many are lost. They are in fact, separated from their Father by sin; the sin of unbelief being the chief sin, responsible for every other kind. But, like the children who are orphans and urchins in your cities, they do not recognize their lostness because they have never experienced 'found-ness'! It's not until a sense of lostness arrives that they can desire to be found. (Incidentally, this is what your scriptures mean when they speak of being '*found,* in him.')[1] Many will be aware of the parable I was later to tell when among you; the one about the 'prodigal' or wayward son.[2] When he returned home, his father said 'this son of mine was lost, but is now 'found.' You see, he became 'found' even though no-one went looking for him! His circumstances caused him to recognize his lostness.

In your case, I, Wisdom am always being sent from the Father, the Elohim One, with words and actions and presence, by which, together with your circumstances, you may become both aware of lostness, and then become 'found'. Particularly with words—with communication, so that I, Wisdom have also become recognized by those of you who know me, as—*the* Word of Yahweh! Your great Psalmist Dawid has said, 'by the Word of Yahweh the heavens were made, and all the host of them by the breath of his mouth.'[3] I will have more to say on this later, but that breath is his Spirit and as you can see from the record of creation, both Elohim's Spirit and his Word were involved in bringing it all forth![4] And—see what Dawid's son, the great Shalomoh said . . .

> 'The Lord **by wisdom** founded the earth;
> By understanding He established the heavens'[5]

But . . . to return to my thrust, yes, I, Wisdom have always been coming to you in every age to make known the mind of Yahweh. We are one Spirit; indeed, as your great prophet Yshai'yah has said, foretelling the coming one, the one also known as the Branch from the stem of Jesse . . .

> 'the Spirit of Yahweh shall rest upon him,
> The Spirit of **Wisdom** . . .'[6]

---

1. Philippians 3:9
2. Luke 15:11–32
3. Psalm 33:6
4. Genesis 1:2 & 3
5. Proverbs 3:19
6. Isaiah 11:2 (emphasis added)

I have already shown you how Yahweh Elohim chose, and I called, the man Avram, who became the great Ivrahim; and from him came, eventually, those called The People, the benei ha Elohim (sons of Elohim).[7]

It was to them that I came also through the great Moshe, with the Word that was to show them their way out of lostness and into being a 'found' people—that is, foundlings.[8] Actually, it was he, Moshe who sang about them being found. Here is part of his song . . .

> *"He (Yahweh) **found** him in a desert land*
> *And in the wasteland, a howling wilderness;*
> *He encircled him, He **instructed** him,*
> *He kept him as the apple of His eye."*[9]

The Word with which I instructed them showed what the Father's heart is like and our desire for our likeness within them. It provided his righteous requirements which, if followed, would bring them into greatness and destiny—would mark them out as different in a way that made I, Wisdom visible and desirable.[10]

To be a reflection

And so it was, that I spoke with Moshe at the bush—and issued Father's call to him and he went, yes hesitantly at first, but with growing confidence to confront the great P'roah of Mitsrayim.[11] And so through him we brought out the people who were to become The People of Elohim. But in order for them to bear the name of Yahweh Elohim they had to understand what we were

---

7. See this author's book 'THE PEOPLE: the sons of God (through the eyes of a Watcher)' Wipf and Stock ISBN: 978-1-5326-4828-1.

8. The little-used English word 'foundling' describes a child abandoned but found and cared for by someone. It well describes those 'found' by their loving Heavenly Father.

9. Deuteronomy 32:10–12 NKJV (emphasis added)

10. Deuteronomy 4:6

11. Egypt

like, for we desired a people in the earth, among all peoples, who were once again a reflection of us. It was necessary for them to see our nature and character and then to see that our call upon them was to reflect us among the Goyim! It was necessary because we always require in your realm a pointer to the life and wisdom that we offer to all who will turn.

I see that in your day an unending succession of laws, legislated by humans (all equally flawed) is required in vain attempts to engender good, or at least improved, behavior. It should be evident by now that this is an endless and somewhat futile endeavor, yet your human legislators continue to believe they are making both you and your world a better place! And to be fair, we see that some have in their heart a genuine desire to improve the lot of those less fortunate or unjustly treated. But if the flawed human heart has all but discarded the simple Ten given through me, why is it that you believe people will be eager to keep tens of thousands?

The ten I gave disclosed just where your lostness lay.

When I gave them, you'll notice they were prefaced with these words, "I am Yahweh your Elohim who brought you out of Mitsrayim, out of the house of bondage."[12] You needed to recognize what I was doing for you by my power and my grace. It was deliverance from a terrible ignominy and lostness, in order to make you into a 'found' people of great purpose.

You had been in the thrall of Mitsrayim because for a long time you had been drifting from me and my ways and now, I was heeding your cries and giving you a marvelous liberation and redemption so that you could walk out of your bondage and lostness. But you had to see that to be found—to become something of truth and usefulness in the earth—required behaving as my 'found' people!

The Ten Words exactly disclosed (as I have said) wherein your lostness lay. They were given so that you could live in 'found-ness.'

You had turned to other gods—those of the Goyim. Such action immediately divided your allegiance. You were (to use an expression of the reader's day because it is still occurring), 'hedging

---

12. Exodus 20:2

your bets' and demonstrating that you doubted me and my ability to do as I had promised. That syncretism immediately took you out of my protection and subjected you to the thrall of the deceitful powers behind those idols.

Of course, that's why the first of those ten words reminded you of who I am and that you are to have no other gods before me! Further, you expected my activity toward you to be on your terms; that you could demand—on the basis of your very limited understanding—my immediate attention to your every imagined discomfort. You showed this distrust by becoming complainers instead of restful believers. Believe me, I was ready to feed you and provide water—indeed, ready to take you right into the land I had promised you. It would have been but an eleven-day walk![13] But you demonstrated that you were not of the right stuff to be in my land—whose maintenance and yours within it—required restful trust. You failed every small test I gave you to prepare you for life within it. You showed yourselves unready for what I had in mind. Alas!

My Ten Words were given so that by adherence to them you could enter into your 'found-ness' in Yahweh—as The People belonging to him and who were seen to belong to him because your behavior (and your heart) was as his! But . . .

You had made your 'gods' of carved images of creatures *I* had made! *You* made them—and then you bowed to them as though I was not there—as though it was *they* who had made you and brought you out! And when you did invoke my name, it was as though I was your servant and then you profaned the day that I asked to be set aside to honor me and to distinguish you as a people who trusted me. You dishonored your parents—those who bore you and nurtured you and you relinquished your obligations to them. You took the lives of others made in my image and thought you could do so with impunity! Like those around you, you made a travesty of marriage and broke its sacred covenant. You lied about others to keep yourself out of trouble or to maintain favor with

---

13. Deuteronomy 1:2

The Person

others. You coveted the goods and houses and wives and possessions of others!

These were all the symptoms of your lostness and separation from me which I addressed in those ten words which would bring you to me and reflect my nature and character. They were simply the expression of my desire to see you live in favor and prosperity.[14]

These ten were all that you needed if your heart had indeed been inclined to me . . .they were Wisdom for you—and were intended to display wisdom to the nations. I said to you, "Therefore be careful to observe them; for *this* is your *wisdom* and your understanding in the sight of the peoples who will hear all these statutes, and say, 'Surely this great nation is a *wise* and understanding people.'"[15]

When Moshe had asked to see Yahweh's glory[16], Yahweh agreed and said, "I will make all my *goodness* pass before you." It is important that you know that his glory, that is, what constitutes him[17]—is goodness! That is why those ten words were housed in the ark of his Presence; they represented what he is like. They were to be housed among you and to become your glory also—the thing which comprised *your* life . . .goodness.

That too, is why the breaking of these words (or the neglect of them) was reckoned as sin,[18] because it caused separation from me. They were given to show the standard and to enable you to return to the likeness to me that you had lost. In your day dear reader, that standard is exactly like the speed restriction signs you have on your highways. When you drive, those signs perform two

---

14. Prosperity meaning all that the Hebrew word shalom embraces in soundness, completeness, well-being.

15. Deuteronomy 4:6

16. Exodus 33:18

17. The Hebrew word KABOD essentially means 'weight' or abundance, that of which a thing is comprised.

18. Three words are typically used in the Old Testament and are all employed in Psalm 51:2&3; PESHA; transgression-to drift across the line; AWON; iniquity-deliberate rebellion, disobedience; KHATTAW; sin-from a root meaning coming short of the standards, missing the mark (as an arrow falling short).

functions: they show unequivocally the required standard and limit—and at the same time condemn you if you are exceeding it!

"But," you cry, "we have all broken them! Who of us has not coveted? Who has not lied or given false witness?"

"How true that is" say I Wisdom, "all have indeed come up short, but Father Elohim has made provision for your falling short and even for your rebellion, to be cleansed! So great is his desire to have you included with us and have you joined with us for eternity.

"His provision was a temporary—perhaps what you would call a 'stop-gap' measure because it had to happen within the constraints of time; blood being spilled to make atonement, constantly reminding you of the seriousness of human departure. But every one of those offerings and substitutes pointed and pointed . . .kept pointing forward—to a completion—a final and efficacious-for-all-time, sacrifice. And the Law pointed and pointed . . .to One who could keep it perfectly in your behalf as your proxy."

CHAPTER 6

Wisdom embedded

Only take heed to yourself, and diligently keep yourself, **lest you forget** *the things your eyes have seen, and lest they depart from your heart all the days of your life . . .*

—DEUTERONOMY 4:9, NKJV

BECAUSE FATHER CREATED YOU within the constraint known as time, and as an analog of Our self, it was necessary for you to be created with the faculty known as memory. It is not yet possible for you to properly comprehend anything other than time, but for us, all events are unconstrained and, in a sense, always extant. Yes, I know this is mystery to you—and tantalizing—but you too are destined for this side; and can be here if and when you complete properly, your sojourn. That is our intent and plan and we long for you to join us here when Time, so far as you are concerned, is discarded—when that construct is no longer needed. In fact, you were created for *this* realm and we have made it possible for you to join us here; or for the two realms to become one in our new creation. It remains for you to avail yourself of our provision.

And yes, back to memory: for it is important for your welfare that you are enabled to look back and recall those things we have done at various and significant points along your Time-line. To help you, Father instituted in the life of The People, various Feasts memorializing our saving and redeeming acts and events. These were pictorial and graphic in nature so that they and their meaning could be repeated and passed down your generations to children and children's children. In this is wisdom.

Rise of the myth-makers

But, this subject of memory leads to another matter, important for you to grasp. As has been said elsewhere, two streams flow along the line you call Time. These are, the stream constituted of those known throughout our revelation as benei adam, the sons of men—and, the stream called benei ha Elohim, the sons of God.[1] The benei adam are those who chose (and continue to choose) to strike off on their own, believing they know better and can manage lives and events perfectly well by themselves. Perhaps, to be more exact, we might say they have 'un-chosen' us.

It is they who, in order to account for the existence of the world (and indeed, themselves) and for the catastrophic and significant cosmic events retained in mankind's collective memory, have become myth-makers. For example, they have found it necessary to invent stories to account for—in a way that excludes Yahweh Elohim—creation and the epic deluge that swallowed the earth.

I, Wisdom have seen this tragic necessity come upon them because of their choice to be independent. If you're going to try to live off to the side on your own, of course you'll have to find a way—an alternative way—of accounting for the system within which you live. And you'll have to invent a kind of purpose and reason or interpret the events that have come down in your collective memory, in fanciful ways. This has led to all kinds of myths such as the Gilgamesh Epic or the Rainbow Serpent of the Australian Aborigines or the Wiracocha myths of your Inca people. They are invented means to try to account for what *we* have performed. Most of these invented systems necessarily devolved to a cyclical or wheel-like philosophy; a fruitless cycle of purposelessness, around and around ad infinitum with no end point or outcome. Futility. It

---

1. See this author's book, 'THE PEOPLE: The Sons of God (through the eyes of a Watcher)' ISBN 978-1-5326-4828-1

is only our followers, the bene ha Elohim—those who have chosen to stay with us, who have the true account and have, through their closeness to me, been enabled to interpret events correctly. I have given them the truth; and it is directional, cumulative, and has a grandly defined purpose and outcome!

Of course, myth-making has not ceased. In your day the same spirit patrols your earth. There are many who are compelled in their independence to account for everything—even their own independence—by myth-making. They have constructed many modern myths to exclude Yahweh's presence. Some of them are more ridiculous than those of the ancients for they, at least posited a being or a force—a cause, but in your day, many want to exclude cause entirely—which of course, makes things even more pointless. Such inventions only serve to show up the desperation of men to avoid accountability and indeed, to make gods of themselves. It is the grand folly, the folly of follies—for which we offer the remedy—Wisdom from above.

But . . . to return to the matter of memory and of my presence among you—

Pointers and Memory aids

Yahweh gave you, the benei ha Elohim—believers in the true story—seven great memorial feasts, each commemorating an important and significant event in your journey with me. These were to have a completion in and through me when I eventually became en-fleshed among you . . . and also in history beyond that! For I, Wisdom am hidden within each of them and all of them, and I am found by searching, as one of your own has said, "you shall seek me and find me when you search for me with all your heart."[2]

We have observed a laziness within the heart of man—sometimes a sense of entitlement; but, as all know, that which is most eagerly or diligently sought becomes the most valued when found. Jewels are sought and found by diligence because they are worth

---

2. Jeremiah 29:13

Wisdom embedded

the expenditure of effort. And so it is, that when I ensure that a heart is truly *for* me—it is then that I disclose myself and meet that heart. A day came when I said this very thing among you, "Keep asking, and it will be given to you. Keep searching, and you will find. Keep knocking, and the door will be opened to you."[3] It is my promise!

You see, my role and heart as mankind's Redeemer was disclosed to The People in Pesach.[4] Then, in Hag Hamatzot[5] I showed that my work was to sanctify you and make you into my own separated and holy ones! I signified, as well as foretold things to come in *all* the feasts I gave you. Why, just look at all these other reminders and opportunities throughout each year to validate and refresh among you my presence and activity in behalf of those called HaAm—The People[6]...

My celebration of Yom Habikkurim[7] was intended to remind you of Yahweh's bounty and grace in the land named as yours, and fifty days later that resounding outburst of joy known as the Feast of Weeks (Hag Shavuot). Oh, and to keep before you the importance of your nation-hood and your peoplehood, you had Rosh Hashana.[8] Finally you had that all important Yom Kippur, the Day of Atonement and then Sukkoth, your festival of Tabernacles reminding you of your days of sojourning and that your life is but a sojourn!

In all these, I, Wisdom was being revealed—for wisdom is always found in mindfulness of the kindness of Yahweh and of all that he has done to demonstrate his nature, not only to you, but through you, to the nations. Ah yes, it is always wisdom to remember his work, to meditate therein, to give thanks...for forgetfulness leads to apathy, apathy to harmful indulgences and to

---

3. Matthew 7:7
4. Passover
5. Unleavened Bread
6. See this author's book 'THE PEOPLE: The Sons of God (through the eyes of a Watcher)'
7. Feast of First-fruits
8. Feast of Trumpets or Blasting.

distance from his favor—and finally, likeness to those to whom you are called to demonstrate difference and advantage! And, that is why in the day of you who read, you are called not to forsake your assembling together to remember and to celebrate my new feast.

CHAPTER 7

History is Mine

> *Blessed be the name of God forever and ever,*
> *For **wisdom** and might are his, and he changes*
> *the times and the seasons;*
> *he removes kings and raises up kings;*
> *he gives **wisdom** to the **wise**...*
>
> —DANIEL 2:20-21

I, WISDOM AM AWARE that there are many who hesitate to enter into trust, or to even begin to move in my direction because they feel that if the Father and I are who we claim to be then surely we would intervene in the sorry mess that they see around them, to make things better.

And we see also that it is indeed a sorry mess. But when people talk of intervention, they clearly have something in mind. A particular kind of intervention; one that delivers justice and alleviates suffering and lack, for example. Or prevents war and conflict.

There is a problem here that I have been at pains to help people see, right throughout your history. For when you say "why does he not intervene?" I, Wisdom must immediately retort, "Intervene? But I have intervened!" And the truth of the matter is that you do not like my intervention because it requires something of you.

Allow me to explain. All through history I *have* intervened! Yes, stepped into the sorry mess to point you to the answer—to Me ...to Us! I AM THE ANSWER! But you have always pushed me away in one way or another, just as I have been saying, you have 'un-chosen' me!

I intervened to give you Ivrahim. I intervened to give you Moshe and Yeshua and Dawid and the prophets. Intervene, you say! Can you be so blind as to *not* see my interventions; my stepping in at crucial moments to lead you to myself?

Whilst all these were in a sense, me, in one disguise or another, the greatest intervention was the taking of flesh to be one of you. We will get to that soon enough.

No, it is not lack of intervention that is the problem: it is your rejection of my interventions. Earlier I told you that the sin called unbelief is the chief sin and now I hope that you will see more clearly what I meant. Many, because of an irrational fear of belief, deliberately and willfully choose UN-belief! For which they seek—and find—a thousand rationales!

History is mine. As some of your own have cogently pointed out, it is 'His-story' and that is indeed the truth. For I form the very warp and weft of your time journey. I am woven into every event—yes, large *and* small—I form and am in charge of the changing of times and seasons, the raising up of kings and rulers. I have ensured that the record shows this in unmistakable clarity and it is, of course, why it is important to read the written-down Word I, Wisdom have provided for you. Therein is your history—as well as things to come—from our perspective: Wisdom written.

It too, in its own way, is another intervention in your life on earth.

CHAPTER 8

Wisdom in Correction and Foresight

WHEN THE GREAT YAHWEH-ELOHIM showed himself to your father Ivrahim on that day-for-the-ages on the mountains of HaMoriyah,[1] he was revealed as The Foreseeing One.[2] Yahweh had seen ahead of Ivrahim with the lamb caught in the thicket and this provided a life lesson for Ivrahim as it does for all who read of the incident. Ivrahim was henceforth able to be confident that this is what Yahweh does for those who obey. It is an unfailing principle. He makes a way where none is visible: he has always gone ahead—is ahead. And of course, this demonstrates that the true way, the way of Yahweh and of the benei Elohim is directional and purposive; is indeed linear, for he is always pointing ahead to purpose and fulfilment and culmination!

Standing as he does, outside of the linearity he created and which you call time, he can see what you call the end—from the beginning! He inserts himself (as it were) at a point ahead, or indeed has me stand there 'where the paths meet' to beckon you forward and onward, on the true path.

So it is that life with Yahweh Elohim is no senseless cyclical vanity! He is always desiring to include you—yes, every one of you—in the journey of history, His-story—the one that culminates. Of course, it will culminate for all the myth-makers and

1. Moriah (see Genesis 22:2)
2. Yahweh Yireh means Yahweh who foresees (in English pro-vide means to see ahead from Latin pro—ahead and vide—to see).

37

myth-believers among you also, but it does not look like a good end. It will be however, the end chosen because in their case, they have 'un-chosen' Truth and Reality.

It is the foresight of Yahweh that provides the ground for trust in him. As humans you possess very limited capacity for foresight—especially since your loss in Edhen through your first father 'Dam. It is the offer of the great Yahweh to be your eyes ahead! But it is for those who will allow him to act thus, and trust him to act thus. Otherwise you walk in blindness and a mist of very limited vision. Those who allow him to be the Foreseeing One, find a peace and a restfulness which, as one of your own has said, 'passes all understanding.'[3] I, Wisdom have seen this come to all who are willing to walk as Ivrahim walked; the great Moshe and Yeshua and Kalev, not to mention the prophets and many of those known as The People—there are so many. But they are all there in the annals he has entrusted to you so that you may seek and find! Indeed, one of your own has listed many of those who walked of old as Ivrahim walked.[4] In this is wisdom.

And so, speaking of the prophets, I want to remind you that they demonstrate this very aspect of Yahweh's wisdom. They are a demonstration of his foreseeing nature and love. To those known as The People, he sent them to signal to you what he was seeing and thereby bring assurance. They saw what he saw, not only in your present, but also for seasons ahead of you. This is why he also called them seers.[5] Can you see what a gift they were (and are in your present day also) to you? They were to be your eyes to keep you from falling into traps or from the pathway, and a light in the dark places. Your walk—your sojourn, is one for which you require 'eyes', albeit eyes of belief. It is saddening for me, Wisdom, to behold that some refused to have eyes and preferred blindness and, as one of these very seers has said, 'to stumble in darkness.'[6]

---

3. Paul In Philippians 4:7
4. See Hebrews 11
5. In Hebrew KHOZEH, a beholder, one who sees, a see-er
6. See for example, Isaiah 59:10

Wisdom in Correction and Foresight

On occasion, because of your disobedience, Yahweh himself closed your 'eyes.'[7] Alas, that is the condition of the heart of those called humankind: sight is offered; blindness is chosen—and sometimes preferred! This is folly indeed—and of a kind that I, Wisdom find to be of great offence.

---

7. Isaiah 29:10

CHAPTER 9

A Zenith in shadow form

*. . .for this will show your **wisdom** and understanding to the nations, who will hear about all these decrees and say, "Surely this great nation is a **wise** and understanding people*

—DEUTERONOMY 4:6, NIV

*Now, O Lord God, let Your promise to David my father be established, for You have made me king over a people like the dust of the earth in multitude. Now **give me wisdom** and knowledge, that I may go out and come in before this people; for who can judge this great people of Yours?*

—2 CHRONICLES 1:9-10, NKJV

IT IS TIME FOR me to show you how I, Wisdom, typified myself in a special demonstration among the people called by the name of Yahweh Elohim—the people known as Ysra'El. For they were chosen and called for this very purpose; that is, to provide incontrovertible evidence in your earth that his wisdom is available. It can be sought, and found. It was to be seen as superior to that of the sons of men. It was to be seen as accessible; yet how could it be seen unless through people—The People?

And so it was; for the nations *did* witness it—and knew. And they spoke of it—some with desire, some with the folly of jealous anger! And from that jealous anger many tried to prove their own superiority by great threats against The People. Alas, if The People

A Zenith in Shadow Form

forsook the One who was Wisdom to them, they quickly became vulnerable.

It is a fact that for all of time the 'wisdom' of the benei adam (the sons of men) has not comfortably comprehended me, the Wisdom from above,[1] for the two arise from very different springs. It is my intention always that the sons of Elohim receive the Wisdom that is from above...receive Me. I am there for the asking! One of your own has described it thus: 'But the wisdom that is from above is first pure, then peaceable, gentle, willing to yield, full of mercy and good fruits, without partiality and without hypocrisy.'[2] You will agree...a beautiful thing; a thing to be coveted and sought. Its opposite is also described and is clearly to be shunned. Here it is: 'This 'wisdom' does not descend from above, but is earthly, sensual, demonic. For where envy and self-seeking exist, confusion and every evil thing is there.' You see, the choice is clear and the same writer wrote these words, 'if any of you lacks wisdom, let him ask the One who gives liberally and without finding fault, and it will be given!'"[3]

My People had to keep choosing, just as you who read must decide—and you must do it now and in fact, every moment thereafter: between sensuality, the demonic realm that fosters narcissism, leading to confusion—or, purity, peacefulness, tractable gentleness with beautiful fruit and without the burden of hypocrisy. Of course, there is a certain 'empowering' that results from either choice, and you must discern the source of each. There is an enemy of all that is righteous, productive and good and whose desire is only destruction and, oh yes, he will seek to facilitate and empower anything to that end...'the thief comes *only* to rob, kill and destroy.'[4] But, I Wisdom, will empower all that is headed in the direction of my life and my love and redemption.

It's what is called in your day a 'no-brainer!' That choice itself, *is* wisdom.

1. James 3:15-16 (NKJV)
2. Ibid
3. James 1:5
4. Jesus in John 10:10

The Person

Yet, it was in and from the House of the one known as Dawid, that I (and indeed, We) came to be most visible to the Goyim. He, Dawid, was one after our own heart and we knew that in him we could establish a lineage. Yes, human and frail he proved to be, as had Moshe and Ahron and all the great ones before him, but always he returned with repentance and sincerity of heart. Always he chose again the path that results in life and blessing. He was, therefore, of the very kind through whom we can do our work—and in doing so, ensure that they receive blessing and honor also! For this is how we love to join with you. It is for this very walk we created you, yes, every one of you. And for you who read—yes, it is so—the walk of co-function; I in you and you in me![5] The best of you see it, embrace it, and come to live and rest in it!

So it was that in the House of Dawid, I came to be seen and indeed magnified, so that nations and kings saw…and wondered. And I, Wisdom, in the purpose and plan of Father, was revealed in an almost new and unprecedented way. For it was the son of Dawid, who, so influenced by his great father and upon coming to the throne, called upon Yahweh Elohim for me to be manifest in him. So conscious was the great Shalomoh[6] of his need, that here is what he prayed upon his ascendency to the throne of his father…

> *"You have shown great mercy to your servant Dawid my father, because he walked before you in truth, in righteousness, and in uprightness of heart with you; you have continued this great kindness for him, and you have given him a son to sit on his throne, as it is this day. Now, O Lord my God, you have made your servant king instead of my father Dawid, but I am a little child; I do not know how to go out or come in. And your servant is in the midst of your people whom you have chosen, a great people, too numerous to be numbered or counted. Therefore give to your servant an understanding heart to judge your people, that I may discern between good and evil. For who is able to judge this great people of yours?"[7]*

5. See John 14:20 and 17:23
6. Solomon
7. 1 Kings 3:7–9

A Zenith in shadow form

That Shalomoh cried out for this pleased the Father-heart of Yahweh Elohim greatly, especially the humility in which he asked. His was the attitude that Father's heart always immediately responds to for it is the attitude of recognition; recognition of place and order and dependence. And so it pleased the Father that I, Wisdom, should inhabit this man—in a way that pointed to something greater. Let me explain . . .

When you stand near the corner of a wall, you cannot see around the corner but (if the light is in the correct place) you may see a shadow emerging ahead of a person before that person comes into view. You know then that the embodiment is about to appear. The shadow does not provide much in the way of detail or color but it does provide certainty that there is movement in a direction and that a real person will soon appear!

Dawid and Shalomoh and others both before and after, were just like that shadow. They alerted you to an approaching embodiment—the coming among you of Myself entirely embodied as one of you! Together with the prophets all these events and people provided a clearer and clearer anticipation of my arrival among you.

What this meant was that The People, during Dawid's and his son Shalomoh's reign, came under our authority and wisdom in the fullest manifestation that the nation, and the world, had yet seen! Indeed, as a consequence, they, and what they possessed and represented became sought after as never before! And, in the way we had always intended! It was indeed a high point, a zenith in the life of The People. I was on display!

With wisdom, the Father also gave abundance, even in those things most admired by the Goyim—honor and wealth of goods and flocks and harvests. But especially was Shalomoh's wisdom so fabled and news-ed abroad that the kings and queens of the earth sent high officials to behold and to see if it were true.[8] The nations' values resided in power, possessions and wealth and their fear was always that one or another nation might be superior to them in these things. But what they beheld was the blessing of Yahweh Elohim upon a people, The People who now honored, revered and

---

8. 1 Kings 4:34

The Person

worshipped him. Oh, it was a time and a season that pleased the heart of the great Yahweh Elohim, whose heart was (and is) indeed for *all* mankind to seek him and to find him and the wisdom that is from above.

Indeed, there was one (among the many), who, as it turns out, can now be seen to represent all of you who read. For she had heard, as had the whole world, of the wisdom of Shalomoh. She came to behold; and her visit speaks. It speaks of our longing for the entire world of men. It speaks of our longing for those known as our own. For, she, the Queen of Saba heard—and came to see, to capture first-hand the truth of Yahweh-among-you—and within the person of the King of Ysra-El![9]

I, Wisdom cannot emphasize enough how this was the very heart of Father—that *all* people seek us and know us, and come to find the completion that flows from that.

And so it was that Shalomoh the Great, typified—in fact exemplified—Yahweh's desire that I, Wisdom reside within The People—co-habiting and co-functioning with them and that I, Wisdom, be sought after by all mankind.

So, Shalomoh's life pointed ahead to a yet greater en-fleshment of Wisdom among you. Indeed, this ideal—this great arrival—was always being spoken of in all of our words and actions among you. It had been spoken in the Ten Words, spoken through the experiences of The People, spoken in the Tabernacle and the Priesthood and the Feasts, spoken by the Prophets and now by the Kings. The true, the ultimate Zenith was arriving—about to appear around the corner—I, Wisdom, was on the way to you in an even more dynamic en-fleshment!

---

9. See 1 Kings 10:1ff and Matthew 12:42

CHAPTER 10

The Promise

> *The Spirit of the LORD shall rest upon him,*
> *the Spirit of **wisdom** and understanding,*
> *the Spirit of counsel and might, the Spirit of knowledge and*
> *of the fear of the LORD . . .*
>
> —ISAIAH 11:2

IT HAD BEGUN FIRST as just an allusion—a hint, as Yahweh Elohim addressed the nachash—the serpent, at the beginning: "He," meaning the Seed, one day to eventuate from the woman, "shall crush your head, even though you will crush his heel." I, Wisdom ask you to consider to whom Yahweh was alluding by using the singular, 'he'? At that very moment a promise was sown; a promise that began to be seen and embraced, over time, as the epicenter of a coming earthquake.

I, Wisdom must remind you—perhaps inform you—of the way The Father reveals what he calls 'secrets' or 'mysteries' to you, his most prized creatures. As we will see much later, his way is to discern among the creatures, those whose heart is inclined to (or inclining toward), him. He always seeks those with ears to hear and eyes to see. You can see that this is the major difference between the benei haElohim[1] and the benei adam.[2] Those with inclined hearts catch the allusions and hints and nuances he uses

---

1. Benei haElohim, those known as the sons of God: See this author's book, 'THE PEOPLE: the sons of God'
2. Benei adam, those known as the sons of men.

to draw them to truth. These are they who please his heart as they respond. Mind you, it is not because he has no care for the others; he is simply at work always to bring them to a place where their ears *will* hear and their eyes, see.

But, to return to my thrust: the truth is, that to all who begin to pay attention to the 'allusions', their 'message' grows in clarity as they progress. It's as though both the message, and the heeding ones, become stronger with passing time. The 'shadow' of the emerging person becomes more distinct . . .yes, it is that of a person, a man; one of you. It must be the One who will be recognized as Messchiach!

It is one of the ways he makes use of time to your benefit. And so it is, that in the record that faithful ones have, under his guiding hand, set down, there is a growing persuasion. From hint to growing emphasis, from repeated emphasis to established promise; from promise to indubitability—producing . . .expectation!

So, from that first hint, as people inclined their hearts to Yahweh, there grew stronger and stronger statements. To Ivrahim through whose 'seed' *all* the peoples of the earth would become blessed; to the great Moshe, that there would arise a prophet like him from among them in whose mouth would be the words of Yahweh. And so, increasing in strength and specificity, the word kept coming until you received the remarkable predictions of King Dawid and of prophets such as Yshay'Yah, "a young maiden shall conceive and bring forth a son . . .Immanu'El— 'El among you'!

You were told that he would be of the house of Dawid and where he would be born and so many details that the expectation became written in the heart of every child of Ivrahim. He was patterned and presented in shadow form in prophet and priest and king among you as well as within the feasts and sacrifices; the shadow, as I told you before, indicating that its substance was about to be revealed in what was called, 'the fullness of time.'

As I have also told you, I was in the great King Shalomoh, bringing the people whom the prophet Yshay'Yah also called 'my servant' to a high point of demonstration to the nations of the earth. My shadow-form was unmistakably there. Despite your

The Promise

many failures, the nations knew, or came to know that Yahweh was truly supreme and that he was the One who worked wonders. And that wisdom was to be found with him! Oh, they witnessed it—and spoke of it and whispered it in their councils—and tried to keep their constituents' confident in their own governments and the gods they espoused. But the stories abounded up and down the trade routes and among the travelers and mercenaries upon whom people waited for news from elsewhere: about the sea that opened and the drowning of the army of Mitsrayim; about the fiery mountain, about the Yarden River crossing and the walled city of Yericho's fall. He made very sure that the nations beheld. Much of the warfare brought against you were vain attempts by others to validate to themselves that their gods were just as great, or greater.

Alas, then there were the failures, when you wandered from me, or went after the folly of man-made gods.

In all this I, Wisdom was there—as we've said—at every crossroads. In the Law-word, in the Priestly and sacrifice rituals, in the Judges and Prophets and Kings, not to mention within the many whose hearts were devoted and loyal to Yahweh, those known as benei haElohim.[3] And my presence among them all was pointing forward with a promise; indeed, they were all part of the promise. It was that I, Wisdom would arrive in a fuller and more comprehensive embodiment; a culmination—the hinge-pin upon which your earth-history turns.

This pointing was ever there for those with ears to hear and eyes to see, as it gathered emphasis and intensity all along the line known as time. In a moment I will have more to say about the difference between your time realm and my realm, but first, allow me to awaken you to some important names by which I have been recognized and described among both The People and also by thinkers and seekers among the benei adam—the sons of men.

---

3. The sons of God; see this author's book 'THE PEOPLE, the sons of God (through the eyes of a Watcher)' ISBN:978-1-5326-4828-1 (Paperback) or 978-1-5326-4830-4 (EBOOK)

CHAPTER 11

MEMRA and LOGOS

> ...the **Word of the LORD** came to Abram...
> —GENESIS 15:1

> For the Lord revealed himself to Samuel in Shiloh **by the Word of the LORD**
> —1 SAMUEL 3:21B

> ...You have magnified Your **Word** above all Your name.
> —PSALM 138:2C

> For the **Word** of the LORD is right and true;
> **he** is faithful in all **he** does
> —PSALM 33:4

IT IS TIME FOR me to make you familiar with my presence within history and in the history of The People in a way that was glimpsed by the prophets of Ysra'El and was (and is) wondered at by the philosophers of your past and present.

For, of course, I, Wisdom have been there since before the beginning of time and it is me who ultimately governs the flow of events that constitute that which you call history. It is those known as benei haElohim,[1] to whom this reality becomes disclosed most readily as they trust us, but also to many of those who seek wisdom

---

1. Sons of God. See this author's book 'THE PEOPLE: the sons of God (through the eyes of a Watcher)'

MEMRA AND LOGOS

but have not yet found me, there is a dawning that history may not just be some futile, circular repetition, but is purposive and linear with an actual destination. They see that, at least, there appears to be a grand communication that appears to cohere and undergird all things.

Some in your day, in avoidance of the obvious, have suggested that the creation they observe is founded on—or is indeed—mathematics, because much of the visible realm can be described mathematically. If you posit mathematics as a cause rather than a Mathematician you have said nothing. Surely that is only like saying that a book is alphabet. And now we are touching on the understanding of one of the names by which I have been known among you and we'll disclose that in a moment.

As I have already said, it is difficult for you to get far enough back to see how it all coheres. It is very much like a huge impressionist landscape painting of your day. When you stand close, all you see is large incoherent daubs of color and brush strokes, but as you retreat, the further from it you stand, the more sense it makes and the picture begins to cohere and make sense, until at a great distance it may appear almost as a photograph of the subject.

In addition to that, from early times we were impressing on you the understanding that Yahweh Elohim and what he says, are in fact, one. Just as *your* words are an expression of you and characterize you, so it is with us. Our words are the expression of our personhood and character.

For those who learn to trust us, something extraordinary occurs. They receive inside, a settled and peace-filled sense of place and purpose within that big picture; a profoundly pleasing sense of 'who-ness' and identity—as well as oneness with ourselves and with our plan. It is the heart-deep recognition of (and settling into) your exact placement and fit within it—even though you cannot see other parts of the picture. It is a coming home to why you are here; to certainty; to peace. Peace, because it is at that home-coming that we meet you and stamp you with your true (and whole) personhood; what you were created for—your place in the whole!

The Person

History's 'Voice'

But let me enlarge more on this principle, this governing and guiding 'voice' that moves time and history to a culmination (yes, even after many re-starts) and in accordance with a divine symphony; for the voice is none other than . . .mine! And now we are talking logic and mathematics—and a Mathematician!

Many are the descriptions used for me in the records that Yahweh Elohim has carefully curated for you. As I, Wisdom have been seeking to make clear, when the Elohim One created, I was the means or agency by which it was effected— 'by the *word* of the Lord the heavens were made.'[2] His motive was love and I was the means. As we have discussed, what you as humans have to say, issues from who you are and so it is with us . . .

You will see that not only have I been described as Wisdom in your Bible; I am referred to as the Seed, as the Prophet, as Immanuel, as the Servant and Living Water as well as lots of other descriptors. But I have also been discovered and disclosed to you as the *Word* of Yahweh! I am, in that sense, the sum of all that he (and we) have to say to you, our most beloved creation—and I mean what we have to say—past, present and future!

We chose and prepared The People, those known as Hebrews for many reasons, not the least of which was that we had blessed them with a human language rich in characteristics by which we could enjoy disclosing our very being and nature to you. And remember too, that the one we chose through whom to raise up The People was a man we called 'friend' because he was one (like King Dawid later) after our own heart. Ivrahim, under our hand, 'got' where we were 'coming from' and became a willing partner in our plan. And to him we disclosed much about our self including some of our self-descriptors such as Yahweh Yireh, the Seeing-Ahead-Yahweh.

At the head of this chapter you read that 'the word of the Lord *came* to Avram.' It is important that you understand that it was I, Wisdom who actually *came*. Avram did not hear a disembodied

2. Psalm 33:6

voice that had no form. No, I showed myself to him as the living and active speech or word of Yahweh Elohim. Avram actually saw an aspect of our Being—that by which we communicate with you.

As your sojourn continued, the family of Ivrahim (as we renamed him) and the nation arising from him, whom we called our own—The People—gained a growing consciousness of our nature and character. That growth in understanding was part of the reason we had called them out—in order to make known both our presence and our quintessence to all humankind. And so we showed our self as Elohim and Shaddai and Yahweh and Adonai as well as names that described how we feel about and behave toward you, our most beloved creatures!

The Voice with a special Name

And, it is now time to show you a special name by which I became known to The People as they walked with me . . .

The People's scribes and scholars set down, under our guidance (and that of the leaders we had set over you), the dealings and the words describing the journey. They were men of Elohim whose hearts were wholly for us and whose desire was to understand, and transmit, our Truth. The language their early scribes used was the language of The People—Hebrew. However, a time came when, largely because of the failure of The People, they lost the language dear to their hearts (and to ours). For when they had spent seventy years as captives in Bavel (Babylon as the reader will know it), the new generation spoke the language of their captors, albeit a closely related language, known as Aramaic. This language became as you would say in your day, the 'Lingua Franca' of many territories. And so those known as scribes, a scholarly class of linguists and interpreters, undertook the translation of the ancient Hebrew scriptures, into the more common language. It is to these men that you owe gratitude because of their deep knowledge of Hebrew thought, language and idiom as well as understanding of covenantal history. They knew us and they were connected in a succession of ethos-transfer from their deep past.

The Person

It was they who translated the Hebrew scriptures into Aramaic and ensured accurate meaning was carried across by means of explanation of words and phrases. You can see this in practical example in the time of Ehzra the scribe and Nechemyah the leader who rebuilt the wall of Yerushalem on their return from Bavel. Ehzra and others read from the Torah distinctly *and gave the sense and explanation* and helped them understand the reading.[3] This was the important role of the Scribe, for translation is not just knowing words but also understanding intended meaning. To be certain of that, the Scribe had to be saturated in the historical context, culture and idiom of the literature and The People, as we worked in and through them to bring our word and our voice to you.

There was a particular word used in the translations and explanations[4] to describe the means by which Yahweh Elohim communicated with The People—and indeed, by which he had created the cosmos.

Because Yahweh Elohim was so exalted and holy, his 'voice' and his communication was understood as being an intermediary. His *word* therefore, was seen and believed in as having actual personhood, described as The Memra (Word) of Elohim.

Since we—and particularly I, Wisdom—was shown as having spoken creation into being, it was clear to the Hebrew mind that the voice, and more particularly the words, had power and energy that released Divine life—'by the Word (Memra) of Yahweh were the heavens made, and all the host of them by the breath of his mouth!'[5] This idea was clearly implicit within the ancient Hebrew and was clarified in the translations and explanations into Aramaic (known as Targums) where the word Memra is employed. The scribes came to understand the Memra as having creating and saving and Covenant-making power!

---

3. Nehemiah 8:8

4. These were called Targums.

5. Psalms 33:6 & 148:5. The Targums for example, paraphrased Genesis 1:6 like this, 'the word (MEMRA) of Yahweh said, "let there be light" and there was light according to the decree of his memra.' And the paraphrase of Genesis 1:1 is 'In the beginning, with wisdom, the Son and Memra of the Lord, created and perfected the heavens and the earth.'

MEMRA AND LOGOS

Do you see, dear human reader, that I, Wisdom was there—and that my people, The People, understood that truth? It was me, as the word and wisdom of Yahweh Elohim 'wording' all things into being as well as 'wording' the trajectory of events! And because we had chosen The People as the means through which our revelation would be made clear to others, their understanding of my role was something we embedded in their heart and life.

It is to be heeded! Indeed, what you learn from the recorded encounters is that I, Wisdom (and Memra) am worthy of worship and service; I may be spoken to and prayed to! Why, as the great king Dawid so pointedly wrote, 'You have magnified your Word above all your name.'[6]

And . . .it was not only among my people that I was becoming known. Because I am recognizable even to those peoples other than The People (though perhaps dimly), they too began to give a name to that principle of underlying order and purpose which they saw as determining creation and history. The Greek people also named it; their name for it was Logos.

You now see how I had been preparing you for my arrival among you in human form . . .The Memra or Word, becoming flesh, as your great Apostle Johannes later wrote in the Greek language, 'in the beginning was the Logos and the Logos was Theos . . .and without him was nothing made . . .and the Logos became flesh and lived among us.'[7]

Soon I will share with you more about how I, Wisdom actually arrived among you; how I became en-fleshed in order to fulfill Father's purpose. Not that I had not been here . . .but this was the denouement, the actualizing of our spoken word, in human form so that there could no longer be any doubt!

---

6. Psalm 138:2c where 'Word' is MEMRA in the Aramaic Targums. In Hebrew it is a similar word. 'Name' here is used in the sense of recognition, reputation or fame.

7. John 1:1 & 14

CHAPTER 12

Wisdom and Time

I MUST NOW ENLARGE more on the difference between your realm and mine. Yours—that of time—is a construct. As I have said, it was intended by Father Elohim and spoken into existence by me as a beautiful expression of Wisdom. I was the expression, the Word—the Memra—and what has also become known as Logos.

But, regarding Time: As the physicists of your day are fathoming, time is like an arrow, travelling only (so far as you are concerned), forward. We decided on this as the best construct for the dwelling of a class of being as like to our self, though in a particle form, as possible. A being created from Father's loving heart, by me, Wisdom.

Time remains a mystery to you for it cannot be recovered. However, it can be, in a sense, redeemed. Yet only by him. This is so that things lost, may be recovered; brought back to you—but only in him. Father's desire for you is life lived forward, trusting him to work with you, for you, and indeed, in you—for a beautiful culmination. He—and We—require your trust. For if you were able to see all that we see, there would be no need for trust. Our relationship must cohere in trust. And that is why life for you is lived forward into what is always unknown. A minute from now you will probably still be reading this and be on the next page . . .but, there is no guarantee of that. Only I, Wisdom and Father Elohim know whether that is to be!

We have ordained that to know us, is to trust us. If you will not trust that we know all, and, more importantly, know exactly the future, then we cannot function together. It is very much like

Wisdom and Time

the intrinsic trust a child in your world has in a parent. The little child is ignorant of many things—dangers, circumstances, consequences—particularly consequences; and hence the child must rely on the parent to provide, to protect, to ensure the best for it and to be 'in' the child's situation with all the knowledge that enables these blessings.

You are called to a life of such trust. Ours is to be a Father-son relationship. We have an outcome in view for you, which, if you will trust, will result in peace-filled fruitfulness, followed by an ushering into our presence forever, bringing with you all that he has achieved within you (as you trusted) there, on earth. An earth which, by the way, is destined for redundancy and replacement with a new one—of the same nature as our world—eternal, timeless! Yes, a new one 'wherein righteousness dwells.'[1]

And so it was, that the substance, of which the 'shadow' had been hinting and then shouting, was to arrive—at a particular point—upon the line known as time.

I was always there, of course, as the one whose voice commanded your time realm into being—created the environment in which it is possible for there to be a past, a present and a future. It is not possible for you, as creatures bound within that realm, to grasp our sphere, which you call eternity. Ours is a realm in which everything is accessible, as though occurring in what you call the present.

You humans often think of eternity as an infinitely long time, but in doing so you are still thinking in a 'time' mindset. Eternity has nothing to do with time. Perhaps an illustration may assist you in getting an idea of the difference. I want you to imagine you are seated in the lounge-room of an old, historic house. Within that room's history and four walls has been a long parade of people and events: important dignitaries, servants, children, grandfathers and mentors, rich and poor, young and old. Matters of weight and trivia have been discussed. I said "have been" because for you, all those events and words have passed; have, for you, vanished, because each new moment and event supersedes the one immediately

---

1. See 2 Peter 3:13

before it. It is a trajectory—travelling in a direction. In my realm however, there is no direction—no vanishing into a past, no supersession by subsequent events. It is as though you are able to sit in that room and continue accessing all that ever occurred or was said or done there. All those things mysteriously remain extant!

Like a raft on a river—maybe . . .

It may help to imagine a river. For you, as you stand somewhere on its bank, it has an upstream and a downstream, but it is a whole river of which you are seeing only one part. If you immerse yourself in the river on a raft with no means of propulsion other than the river you will begin to flow downstream with it, at its speed. You will not be able to go faster to get ahead of your spot in the river, nor will you be able to propel yourself back upstream. You've become part of the river. Your place in time is like that; it is flowing, and you with it. You can of course, do things within your raft; you might paint or draw or create things, and, if you can imagine a raft large enough, on a river large enough, you may have lots of other people with you with whom to interact and enjoy the journey. The kings and queens of England had whole orchestras and choirs on barges floating down the Thames on occasion.

I, however, for the sake of illustration, am more like an amphibian who can choose to swim within the river or move outside the river and observe it, as I please (and from wherever I choose). Within the river, I may choose to swim down-river faster than its velocity and be (as it were) ahead of your raft 'event' within the river—or I may swim upstream, or indeed across the stream—anywhere I please to go within that flowing stream is mine.

In your day you are, because of your technology, able instantly to access in present time, at least the images of events that occurred in your past. You may view a sporting event or a wedding that was held a week ago . . . or ten years ago. In a sense, the event is residing, unchanged 'out there' ready to be accessed at any moment, in your 'now.' In your case, the events are but in image form, held in one type or another of memory, but let's call the realm in which all those events still (in a sense) reside—eternity. You reside or are locked into your present moment, yet are able to access something past, unfortunately in your case, not in reality. But in my case, the event is actually accessible because it has not passed away! And, more than that, I am able to access events that are yet to appear to you.

All of this is to get to a special point.

Trust

Why were you made to live in the 'time' realm? This moment-to-moment realm? And to this question there is a very special answer . . .

For you see, you were made to learn trust of a particular kind. Let me explain.

Not being able to see ahead is both purposeful and beneficial for you. For that uncertainty is designed to elicit from you a preferred response; it is an opportunity for choice. That uncertainty will cause you either to attempt to create your own certainty—or to receive it from my realm where it abounds!

And what I, Wisdom see, is that many of you try to draw it from the same temporal and uncertain world of which you form a part. For example, some make extraordinary effort to accumulate money and goods to diminish or remove uncertainty whilst others believe it will be removed by popularity and recognition or human adulation, or even by various kinds of questionable prognostications! Yet any of these things are temporary and are no foundation for trust. You can't put your weight down on them because they know nothing of their future either!

Let me remind you of your father Ivrahim, who became ready and willing to relinquish the very thing that appeared certain to secure what Yahweh had promised. Yahweh Elohim called him to trust him *instead of* the apparent 'certainty.' What a lesson it was for Ivrahim—and via him—for every one of you. For it was a principle being demonstrated and when Ivrahim arrived at that place (The Place) in the hills of Moriyah he discovered that Yahweh had arrived ahead of him and prepared the ram for an offering. Ivrahim called him 'Seeing-Ahead-Yahweh' or 'Pro-vision-Yahweh.' Trust was rewarded; trust that was no longer in what Ivrahim could see, but in what Yahweh Elohim could see.

That is the deep thing that I, Wisdom require you to see—and wish to help you see. You are here to learn trust in me, in us! For that and that only, will provide the certainty you seek—and actually need. It's in us and always must be. We know you can't see what we see and hence, in grace, have provided the means for you to know a different kind of certainty. Not in things seen, but simply in our seeing *for* you!

The question is, will you do it? Ivrahim and those who followed (and follow) in his footsteps arrive in a condition we have provided, called rest. It's the place where *we* take all the weight off! Of course, I, Wisdom will have more to say in a little while about this—as I did so fervently when among you—and some of you now know what I am alluding to.

It is the only real answer to your dilemma of living within Time without being able to see ahead! We designed it so! And—we desire that you *enjoy* it!

CHAPTER 13

The Denouement[1]

The seed is the Logos . . .
—LUKE 8:11

WHEN YAHWEH SPEAKS, WHAT he has spoken (through me) carries within it the propensity to materialize—become substance—in accord with his desire. It is analogous to a seed planted in soil: everything that it is to become is within that seed. All that has appeared in every visible and invisible realm, has done so as a result of his desire and will, expressed through me, through Logos.

Of course, in using terms such as breath and voice and words, we do so expressly so that you will get the idea because you have breath and voices and words. You are aware that your own voice and words, although now greatly diminished, retain still a vestige of the power they once held. For with a word you are able still to create. Your words can create pain or jealousy or dismay, or indeed, encouragement, warmth and blessing. Your voice and words still have creative power, though much diminished, because Yahweh's analog within you has been corrupted. That's why, when anyone of you chooses to join with him—with us—one of the first things we change is your 'voice' and your words so that you begin to speak as we speak! When we speak, it is always to lift and to bring help and blessing, never to diminish

---

1. Denouement means the part of a play or narrative in which the strands of the plot become drawn together.

The Person

or harm. Even if we should find it necessary to speak firmly to you, the objective is ever, always only your good!

And so it was that in the same way as we spoke worlds and universes into actuality, it also became necessary to speak rescue into your fallen state. And that we began to do as soon as the consequences of 'Dam's sin became evident. Oh, if you knew how our heart was grieved by your choice in Edhen, even as we began the task of speaking a new creation into reality! Such was our pity and feeling for your now pitiable condition from which you had no way to repatriate yourselves, that a way back was immediately initiated.

Unlike the first creation which occurred in a moment of your time, this new one does have an unfolding. Its evolution had to be along the line you call time, which we had created for you to live within. It has been for you an unfolding revelation of our 'chesed'[2] commitment to you. To put it in its simplest 'time' terms, what was in our heart for you, we began to speak into being. And so, I, Wisdom through time, spoke and spoke and spoke some more; through a person who became a people, through our Law-Word, through a land, through prophets, through priests and kings, through feasts and memorials—always with the intention that eventually, the Word spoken, the Memra and Logos would actualize in flesh and be among you.[3]

And when that happened you saw, first hand, that with which we are full; you beheld one *full of* grace and truth.[4]

Glory

You'll recall as I, Wisdom showed you earlier, that father Moshe once asked to see our glory[5]. . .and what did we show him? Yahweh Elohim said to him, "I will make all my *goodness* pass before you" because 'glory' is that of which a thing is comprised. Glory is

---

2. CHESED, Hebrew meaning Covenant loyalty, lovingkindness, faithfulness.

3. See John 1:14

4. Ibid. 'we beheld his glory . . .*full of* grace and truth' (*emphasis* added).

5. Exodus 33:18. Hebrew KABOD is from KABAD meaning weight or substance; that of which a thing is comprised.

The Denouement

not radiance; no, radiance is the outshining, the manifesting of a thing's glory! The glory of your nearest star, that which you call the Sun, is the mass of fiery gas and nuclear reaction that comprises it. Its *radiance* is the warmth and light that flows from its glory, to your benefit. Just so, the Memra/Logos/Word becoming one of you has been described by one of your own like this, "the Son is the *radiance* of God's glory..."[6]

Hence it was, that I, Wisdom—that statement of who we are and where we are 'coming from' and which many also framed as Logos[7]—came among you exactly as promised, to show you the way through and into the new creation we are delivering. As I have already shared with you, the shadow and hint—the emerging Word of Wisdom—became clearer and stronger as time proceeded, until it became, as it were, a shout, when I, Wisdom stood among you—as one of you!

---

6. See Hebrews 1:3: DOXA in the New Testament corresponds to KABOD in the Old.

7. See John 1:1 etc.

CHAPTER 14

Man in grey meets Wisdom in White

As those of your day are inclined to say, "it was not a pretty sight." Having spoken and spoken and spoken, it was time for all that I, Wisdom had been saying in behalf of Father, to materialize. For as I have pointed out, what Father Elohim speaks, has within it the power to bring into being that which he has spoken, whether event or material entity. It is a principle, another of those secrets that had become clearer and clearer through your history. For you had seen over and again what occurs when he has instructed or spoken. The river Yarden stopped when, at his word, the feet of the priests began to step into its water; the widow's flour and oil did not run out when she obeyed the word of Yahweh through the prophet.

The fullness of Time

Just so, he had been speaking of an *arrival* among you for a long time, but this was different because it had been withheld, embodied in promise, awaiting a fullness of time. It was to 'come to pass', as your writings so often say, at a specific point along the line called time. Not a moment too soon nor too late, only when the 'fullness of time had come.' Those of the reader's time will remember the record of the angelic words to Zechary'yah the father of that one known as Yohannes the Baptizer, 'for my words will certainly be

Man in Grey meets Wisdom in White

fulfilled *at their proper time*.[1] Our word and our words are what cause events—and cause them at the very moment intended.

So it was that the most significant event of your history; indeed, the most extraordinary and compelling, 'event-uated', that is—came to pass!

For I, Wisdom, incarnated: touched down. I, Wisdom, also recognized as the Memra and the Logos of Elohim came among you—no longer in disguise, no longer just as words on parchment or as the voice of law or prophet—but as one of you—yes, human! Materialized in time; en-fleshed like every human before and since . . .as a babe born in the usual way—of woman! Yes, the Logos by whom the cosmos was made and through whom all things exist and are continuously sustained, arriving as one of you! The Word spoken and spoken . . .became flesh in order to *live* among you![2]

It was so that you could behold, firsthand what we are full of . . .grace and truth! Yes, for that is our glory[3] . . .grace and truth!

Disruption

As you can imagine, this coming-as-one-of-you was disruptive! And why? Because it showed you just what 'Dam and every last one of you, was really intended to be like—and indeed, how far you had become removed from that glory.

For I arrived as it were, as a second 'Dam, but now involved in the business of rescue. Of redemption . . .the un-doing of what had become of you. I'll tell you more of that in a moment, but I mentioned that the arrival was disruptive and I need to explain further, for many of those born of that first 'Dam are inured to the horror of how distant they have become from that first and momentarily, ideal one.

You see, when whiteness appears, grey is disclosed for what it is, as when the Fuller of Biblical times whitened linen. Until the

---

1. See Luke 1:20
2. John 1:14
3. Glory (doxa in the NT) is that which fills something; its quintessence, what constitutes it.

contrast appears there is ignorance, but as soon as it is there, it can be neither denied nor dismissed. And that is what happened when I (and We) arrived among you.

As always, the response was twofold; to loathe and shrink away...or, to desire and draw near. Rather like a dark room inhabited by cockroaches and moths when the light is suddenly shone in. The creatures that love and prefer darkness scurry quickly to the darkest corner to escape light, but the moths will be drawn to the light. As your history discloses, those who hated the fact that *The* Whiteness showed up their own grey and unattractive drabness, made it their business to try to rid the world of this intrusive and, in the view of many, unnecessary and embarrassing Light! As one of your own has written 'and this is the crisis, that Light has come into the world, and men *loved* darkness rather than light because their deeds were evil.'[4]

And it therefore became incumbent upon the drab grey sons of men—those fleeing the light—to eradicate this disrupting Logos Wisdom and its burning White-Light. Yes, it was not only White showing up grey; it was Wisdom showing up folly! So powerful means were found—of course, ironically, means that served only to further demonstrate folly. Wisdom-among-you, and so much resented, could easily be pilloried as a blasphemer, or as a worker of wonders by the powers of demons—or as a threat to civil order. As one of the great prophets you were given, so sagely said, "Woe to those who call evil good, and good evil; Who put darkness for light, and light for darkness; Who put bitter for sweet, and sweet for bitter!"[5]

Forever this has been what the folly of grey mankind has done when the Whiteness of Wisdom is shone in. The prophets have truly said to you, "And the Lord has sent to you all his servants the prophets, rising early and sending them, but you have not listened nor inclined your ear to hear."[6] Not to mention that the Whiteness

---

4. See John 3:19 (*emphasis* added. The Greek word translated 'judgment' or 'condemnation' here is KRISIS).

5. Isaiah 5:20

6. Jeremiah 7:25; 25:4; 26:5

Man in grey meets Wisdom in White

as Wisdom-among-you repeated it, "I send them prophets and apostles, and some of them they will kill and persecute."[7]

It has forever been the way.

So, as we have said, it was not a pretty sight, the sight of darkness exposed and contriving to snuff out the Brightness of Wisdom among them. The Light showed up all kinds of dark folly; deceit, hypocrisy, manipulation, greed, self-interest, envy, pride and arrogance, malice, not to mention treachery!

---

7. Luke 11:49 Note this verse says in full, 'Therefore *the wisdom of God* also said, 'I will send them prophets and apostles, and some of them they will kill and persecute,'

CHAPTER 15

Darkness comprehended it not

(JOHN 1:5 KJV)

THE KIND OF DARKNESS of which Apostle Johannes spoke is that which resides in the inner recesses of men's hearts and is loved. It is a darkness which abhors light; it is a folly which abhors wisdom. Its reaction therefore to light is to attempt to subsume it and extinguish it. The beloved apostle—who beheld that Light and embraced it—has told you that it shined . . .arose, *within* the darkness! There I was, at the behest of Father, as the prophet also had foretold—

> *The people who walked in darkness*
> *Have seen a great light;*
> *Those who dwelt in the land of the shadow of death,*
> *Upon them a light has shined.*[1]

There is nothing worse than that death-like shadow that has cast its grim and oppressive pall over the sons of men. It is a shadow that is upon all and which deadens every heart. Of course, it may not be recognized as that because it is all that has been known. And that is exactly why I came, as Light, so that what had been missing might be seen and embraced and lived in and danced within!

It is quite clear that Yahweh Elohim desired Wisdom to be a hallmark of The People who represented him in the earth-realm. It's why he sent his expectations of them in the form of the Ten Words and said, 'for this is your *wisdom* and your understanding

---

1. Isaiah 9:2 NKJV

in the sight of the peoples . . .who will say, "surely this great nation is a *wise* and understanding people . . . ."[2]

His word and his wisdom as we have been so eager for you to see, are one. It is I, Wisdom, who stood behind all the words and events in the long history of my people, awaiting the fullness of time; when I would be manifest in the fullest possible way, among you.

The Word that is Wisdom, at last, on earth. Human!

Of course, the darkness was offended; the folly was shamed. For here stood all the Wisdom and the Light of eternity, suddenly and confrontingly. Here stood the One who made all things, unrecognized by and among, the things and the beings I had made.

When Johannes wrote that the darkness did not comprehend me, he stated profound truth, for his meaning was that the darkness was powerless to overwhelm me or extinguish me. Light and Wisdom, in the end—and at The End—prevail. The One I call Father demonstrated that supremely in me. In fact, that was one of the reasons for my presence among you; to conquer that ultimate darkness and folly you had chosen—known as death.

You must see that death is a product, actually *your* product. The dividend that accrues from your choice. You knew that when you made that choice, yet went ahead. For when you chose that 'other' tree, you deliberately 'un-chose' Life! Became lost to it; and lost to Wisdom.

Many, many in your day are making the same mistake. They've become satisfied in the dim half-light in which they've always functioned, as do some cave-dwelling creatures. They're 'making do' and neither believe in nor desire, anything different or better—and have learned to resent Light because it reveals what they'd prefer not to know; that they are sub-normal.

What is Normal?

I came among you as The Normal; what humanity was intended to look like! Hence the disruption. Most who looked at me saw

---

2. Deuteronomy 4:6 NKJV (*emphasis* added)

something other than just my human form. They saw a very great space between their own heart with its behaviors, thoughts and attitudes—and mine! Naturally, resentment, envy and rage were frequently the response.

Ironically, they were seeing, not so much myself and my light but were seeing their own darkness and their own folly. Take those whose hypocrisy I had to expose and call out—those self-righteous sticklers for every jot and tittle of their religious law. Their 'light' was slavish and showy adherence in the belief that the 'hoi polloi'[3] would fall about with wonder and admiration at their righteousness and holiness! It was a contrived farce, which sadly exhibits itself in every age, including your own as (some of) the men of religion strut about in fancy dress which some imagine provides a statement of their authority and authenticity. Of course, what many of these miss, is that I wish to provide true authenticity and authority that does not arise from externals but from within; from my evident presence and rulership within the lives of those I call as spokesmen and leaders. It is the heart that I see and examine—and change!

It is exactly why I said of them and to them in my day among you, "if therefore the light that is in you is darkness, how great is *that* darkness?"[4]

Our intent was neither to harm nor belittle. Our intent was only that the true Light and Wisdom be seen by means of contrast, recognized as superior—and hungered for. And many did hunger for it . . .and followed, Light.

And many still, in your day, hunger for it and are following it.

---

3. Greek for 'the many'— the common people; hoi polloi has come into English usage as an expression for the masses.

4. Matthew 6:23 (NKJV *emphasis* added)

CHAPTER 16

Among you!

He was in the world, and the world was made through Him, and the world did not know Him. He came to His own, and His own did not receive Him. But as many as received Him, to them He gave the right to become children of God, to those who believe in His name

—JOHN 1:10-11

WHEN WE SAW CHAVEH and 'Dam 'un-choose' us by choosing the proscribed tree in the garden, we knew that intervention from our side was inevitable. Of course, we know that this all constitutes deep mystery to you, but we also know that if you will trust us, you will, in the end (and indeed after the end), see! Your eyes will indeed be opened in *that* day. As one of your own has so truly said 'you will know in the same way as you are known'![1]

Our desire, as we have said, was to set you up as beings as analogous to us as it was possible for you to be, without creating a being for whom choice was not possible. That would be to make you nothing like us at all! Yes, we speak a mystery, as I have said— a mystery only dimly seen as your great apostle said, 'an enigma seen dimly through a glass'[2] but we will have, eventually, a people like us, because they have chosen aright—chosen Me, chosen Wisdom. That is our objective.

---

1. 1 Corinthians 13:12 '. . .I will know completely, in the same way as I am completely known.'
2. Ibid.

And to achieve that and eventually have the people in our likeness whom we first desired, we of course had to intervene. Your history became the story of our great intervention, to redeem. As we told you earlier, we see that some in your day consider the sorry condition of your world and they even say, 'if God cares why doesn't he intervene?' They remain blind to the truth of our intervention, or deliberately reject it.

Immersed in the mess

But what I wanted to say was this: those who govern you in your civil arrangements often act with compassion when there has been some natural disaster among you such as famine, fire, flood or catastrophe. And among the first acts of those who govern is to arrive at the scene of the disaster to be among the devastated, to mourn with those who mourn and to assess what must be done to restore and, where possible, redeem life for those affected.

This, of course, is what we did. We had to be among you. And we began to make ourselves known as an 'Elohim-among-you' even from the first consequences of your disaster—even though it was brought about by your own hand. We love you! We felt your pain more deeply than you can know—especially as we knew there was no way back for you without our intervention.

The story we have been telling you is the story of that intervention. We hope that this time, if you are among those who've not seen it before, will see and begin to receive, Truth. And Wisdom!

You must understand, if possible, the enormity of my arrival and of its impact both on you and on us. There is, as the prophets have said, 'nothing too hard' for us—but for the Logos/Memra, I, Wisdom to become one of you required a far-reaching and humanly unfathomable relinquishment. Physicists of your day grapple with the utter complexity of your cosmos's structure and nature. It too is quite beyond human comprehension as the science of your day tries to come to terms with what is called the quantum realm. But my en-fleshment among you is of far deeper and far more unfathomable mystery than that! It is an act of our realm, an act of the Spirit and cannot be defined at all in any terms satisfactory to the human mind.

But there I was. Among you just as human as you who read. Subject to every human sense and feeling; tempted and tested in every way you have been. Yes, a new start for mankind . . .a new 'Dam, but brought in via a new seed, infused, not with the heritable flaws of 'Dam, but from above. New seed for a new start—a new life, which we wanted to make available to all. The old 'seed' had to be put to death so that the new seed could be made available. That is what I was doing.

Simple, but not easy

I told you it was deeper than human comprehension or capacity, and, because of that, a brand-new way had to be introduced by which this new seed could take effect and reproduce its fruit. It was simple; very simple, yet for some, not easy—but that is where we are willing to help. For it is received by believing that the seed is in me; that it can be received into you by receiving me. Of course, to do that means that you must arrive at the place where you are prepared to let the 'other' life go, by which I mean the self-life, the independent-of-me, prideful life; the 'in- 'Dam-life.' To call *it*, your old life. For the transaction consists of letting the old and inferior go to receive the new and superior. That action is effected by faith and once your mind is made up, I will help you with faith from myself.

(I want you also to see the ramifications for us in making the transaction possible for you. In my case I had to deliberately make myself of no reputation to take among you the role of servant-of-all and then continue to humble myself not only in servanthood, but to complete the commission Father had given me. It required death among you—and at your hand—as the Lamb of God who takes away the sin of the world![3])

---

3. Philippians 2:5–9 & John 1:29 'behold the Lamb of God which takes away the sin of the world.'

But to return to my theme. Among you and as one of you I experienced everything that is experienced by every human who has ever lived. And by that, I mean all those things both good and bad; like disappointment, sorrow, physical agony, mental anguish, hunger, thirst, popularity, rejection and the spitting venom of those who hated my message and my words. I knew the love of human family—and I knew also their misunderstanding and even attempts at manipulation.

But, being among you as both the Light and the Wisdom from Father's realm was the contrast that was the most stark. For I stood among you representing all that 'Dam had lost and has been missing in all since him—and now present again for you to see at close quarters.

It was that which most offended. So practiced had people become at establishing a 'right-ness' of their own—that which ends up calling wrong, right and right, wrong—that *the* true Righteousness appearing among them was more than many could bear! It was like the light of a candle, being considered good and adequate by many, suddenly shown as utterly inferior by the light of the sun! The consequences were sad, but inevitable; 'away with him' became their cry.

Who I Am, now . . .

I looked out upon the world and upon you then, through my human eyes—and still do! For things are altogether different now because I returned to our realm as human; the first-fruit of a new and different category of humankind. I, Wisdom now (figuratively) sit at Father's right hand carrying the scars of my sojourn among you and interceding in your behalf! Yes, in behalf of you who read! Remember this, dear reader, when you are under duress or testing; there is no testing that you undergo that I have not experienced and cannot assist you with—if you will turn and ask! I now not only intercede for you but the Father also sends his Spirit to you to empower and delight.

In fact, it is just as in the first creation when the Elohim *breathed* his life and an 'I am' into 'Dam. Now, in this new creation he again brings you to new life with that same breath.

And, you must not think it was easier for me whilst I was among you because of who I am. Oh no! For I relinquished privilege in order to be one of you.

"But" say some of you, "You had power for miracles and to see the thoughts and intentions of people and even to expose their inmost thoughts," but that was not something I carried with me from outside. No! Rather, as a human, I showed you how to fully submit to our Father and what it was like to have his Spirit come upon me in power to gift me and to enable me. You will recall how I submitted to the baptism of Johannes—a baptism of repentance. In that act, I showed that the attitude *every* human must have before our Father is that of humility and a heart of repentance. I did this as example for everyone, even though I had not inherited 'Dam's corrupted nature—and you'll remember what occurred after that? Our Father sent *upon* me his Spirit, Holy Spirit to equip me for ministry *as a human* among you and to you. That was how I went and it is how you must go.

Do you see that I was showing you how it is to be done; how light and wisdom is to be extant in the world in which you live? The miracles were his work in me and through me as has been recorded for you by Lucas that dear saint of mine, 'how God *anointed* Jesus of Nazareth with the Holy Spirit and with power, who went about doing good and healing all who were oppressed by the devil, for God was *with* Him.'[4]

The prophet had said, 'The Spirit of the Lord shall rest *upon* him, the Spirit of *wisdom* and understanding, the Spirit of counsel and might, the Spirit of knowledge and of the fear of the Lord . . .' and here I was, among you, anointed. I, the very one who had been known as Wisdom, having laid aside what was mine by right and now having to receive it by faith as any other human—dependent now on our Father's gracious sending of the Spirit upon me!

---

4. Acts 10:38 NKJV. All that Jesus did was done as a man anointed by Holy Spirit.

Looking out through flesh-and-blood eyes I could so clearly see a world desperately in need of what I was showing them; demonstrating to them that the same life was possible in each one of them! The presence of our Father's Spirit within and upon each one to enable them to live as I was living within a cosmos out of balance. A cosmos awaiting this very thing—the answer to its imbalance and failure. I, Wisdom was making—creating in fact—the way back! But this work required an undoing; it required the annihilation of the two follies which had beset mankind at the first disobedience—Sin and Death. The latter was the consequence of the first and the unavoidable outcome of the first was the second!

And now?

I must urge my beloved, those now known as my brothers and sisters[5] to live in the same way—to embrace my Spirit, yes, the Spirit of Jesus—whom I and the Father continue sending and making available. Only by embracing me in him will the Light shine; will the same works be done and will the darkness be shown for what it is. Only by us will Wisdom be manifest within a world of folly.

But oh, our heart yearns! For in your day when folly abounds, it saddens us that so much folly also abounds among you, who should know better. The folly of divisions. The folly of my Church compromising my word and my wisdom. The folly of nominal instead of whole-hearted acceptance, both of my joy or my stigma! The folly of acquiescence!

Have you forgotten what it cost to enable you to be as me? Have you forgotten that your role is to be as me to the world? And more to the point . . .how will I, Wisdom, address this folly even among those who wish to name my name? Shall I need to send difficulty and persecution to sift you?

---

5. Hebrews 2:11b

CHAPTER 17

Salvation: Wising up!

The LORD'S voice cries unto the city, and **wisdom shall** *see your name: Hear the rod, and who has appointed it.*

—MICAH 6:9, KJV 2000

Then I saw that **wisdom** *excels folly as light excels darkness*

—ECCLESIASTES 2:13, NKJV

. . .that from a child you have known the holy scriptures, which are able to make you **wise unto salvation** *through faith which is in Christ Jesus.*

—2 TIMOTHY 3:15, KJV 2000

A COMMON EXPRESSION IN your day is 'wise up' used as an injunction to someone to recognize and move away from, folly. In my appeal to you, I, Wisdom call—and those who choose me immediately begin to act more wisely. To heed my beck and call will immediately distinguish the greatest fool as wise! That is why it has been written, 'the fear of the Lord is the *beginning* of wisdom.'[1] The arrival at a reverence of me that leads to heeding me is what we desire—and require. This is what you have been made for.

We recognize that it is a struggle for so many of you because you have been born into cultures (of both macro and micro scale) of those who have practiced (and even raised to an art form) the

---

1. See Psalm 111:10; Proverbs 1:7; 9:10 and Job 28:28 where the Hebrew word is RESHITH meaning 'chief' or 'head', 'foundation.'

75

'un-choosing' of me! And, not content with that, some, hating the sound of my voice have lifted theirs in outrage and clamor against me! They are strident in trying to make disciples, not to wisdom but to folly. The result is folly multiplied and of course this is why we have called and commissioned those who choose us, to declare wisdom and make disciples to us. It is a great battle: Light against gloom; Wisdom against folly.

In your extraordinary age there is much knowledge but there is little wisdom and of course this is because even great minds are starting from the wrong place. They begin with reverence for man instead of awe of us. Some even stand in awe of the Cosmos, yet not of its Origin. The doctrine is called Humanism, the vaunting of man's ability as though it can answer every difficulty and problem. We have permitted your search for knowledge (what you call Science) to result in much that is beneficial. What some fail to recognize is that these benefits, say in medicine and technology have accrued as a result of a grace from us. We are offended when you neither acknowledge us nor express gratitude to us in this! Some in those disciplines are well-motivated, self-effacing and genuine about finding means to alleviate ills and suffering. Their heart is much closer to mine than those who compete for recognition or kudos from the world and their peers. When men begin with reverence for us and proceed from there in their quests, they proceed both with, and toward, wisdom.

Much of the motivation at the deep-heart level for some of the knowledge-seekers, is an answer which they desperately hope will exclude us—even relegate us to the 'dustbin' of history. Ironically, the history of which I am supreme Governor! There is, among some of them, a desperation for an answer that might obviate any requirement for accountability to their Creator and Sustainer. If it can be shown that the word that I have disclosed to you is but a human invention then the only 'truth' is what men decide upon and promote. Hence the extraordinary expenditure of time, energy and life to structure an alternative in which humankind can all trust.

Salvation: Wising up!

That is both folly—and vanity! Its well-spring is a sadly corrupted and self-centered heart; the heart of 'Dam—the heart that un-chose, and continues to un-choose, me!

Our heart's desire is that you see and embrace Truth in us. You can see of course, that this requires a turning; a self-humbling and laying aside of man-pride. You can see also that, as I have said, the 'culture' into which some have been born is that of unbelief toward me; of indifference toward me or ignorance of me. A culture in which only the doctrines of man have been imbibed and heartily embraced. And so often this is because Truth has been suppressed for the very reasons given above.

Hope!

However, for those who follow the desire created by the hollowness in their heart—the hollow place where I should dwell—there is great hope. It begins with a turning. A tearing away from the high-sounding narrative of the Humanist rhetoric to a consideration that Truth may come from *outside* a disgraced and fallen world. Yes, from my Word of Wisdom to you; my word, which as our great apostle told you, has within it the Life and ability to *'make you wise* unto salvation.'[2]

I, Wisdom reside therein. I, Wisdom await you. All you who seek wisdom may only come by the way of humility. Human knowledge will not get you there: cannot get you there. To subject yourself to my way is wisdom indeed.

Thereby fools become wise and folly is seen for what it is.

---

2. Paul in 2 Timothy 3:15

CHAPTER 18

The House that Wisdom built

> ***Wisdom** has built her house . . .'*
> —PROVERBS 9:1A

AND SO IT WAS dear reader that not only did I, Wisdom arrive in your midst and offer up my life in exchange for yours—but I then went on to build a new house on earth. A place in which I could dwell and from which I could minister. This house also had a 'type' and shadow in the Old Covenant (the Covenant that my coming and activity in your behalf, completed). For I dwelt in those days *in the midst of* my people Ysra'El, yes, in a specially prepared 'house' where I 'tabernacled' among them! Within it was the Most Holy Place wherein was my Law-Word of Wisdom for you beneath the wings of the kheruvim and where the High Priest alone could enter but once a year, with blood. The People encamped around my presence with the sure knowledge that I was the central Reality among them, making a way for them. Much later, after the wanderings and settling in the land we gave them, that tent was given permanent form in the Temple built by Shalomoh within Tzion.[1]

When I built that first House, the Tabernacle of Moshe, so that I could dwell and presence myself in the midst of you, it was a work of wisdom. I, Wisdom was there, intimately involved.

Hear how my servant Moshe responded to my command to build me such a place . . . 'Then Moses called Bezalel and Aholiab,

---

[1]. See this author's book 'THE PLACE HaMakom: where Jerusalem's temple stood'

and every gifted artisan *in whose heart the Lord had put wisdom, everyone whose heart was stirred, to come and do the work.*[2]

The more permanent house built later by Shalomoh too, was a work of wisdom for he was chosen by us for that reason. All that I build is a work of wisdom. Alas, it was later destroyed because of the unfaithfulness of The People and when I stood here among you, another like it was still standing right there, in Tzion. However, it too was becoming redundant for *The* Presence now lived and walked among you, albeit briefly. That is why I referred to myself as '*this* temple'[3] for within me was all the presence of Yahweh Elohim! But there was another temple, yet to come.

What you must see is that with me among you in human flesh, all that Yahweh Elohim is, was there, in human form—and when the Father sent the Spirit *upon* me at the Jordan, it was a special picture for all humankind. For I was sent as a man among you—and as a man I needed what everyone who would follow me needs in order to fulfill what We require of them. For those who follow are called to a very great task . . .nothing less than continuing what I had begun in bringing my government to the lives of people who have lost their way.

This I have already said, yet it requires much emphasis: there are those among you who believe that I, Wisdom among you, the Logos made flesh, was able to do the things I did because of who I was: that I brought all of 'that' in with me. But that is not quite true. It's true that I was God among you, but it is also true that I had laid aside much to which I might have laid claim as one of our great apostles has revealed (from us) to you.[4]

It is of utmost importance that you see that my coming to you—and more particularly my ministry accomplished among you—was as one of you—as a man. For I was the progenitor of the new breed, the new creation of mankind. Not only did I need to make a way through your problems of sin and death, but also to

---

2. See Exodus 36:2

3. In John 2:19 Jesus said 'destroy *this temple* and in three days I will raise it up'

4. See Philippians 2:6–8

demonstrate what is possible for New Man! I accomplished all that I did among you . . .*as a man*; yes, a man, a person, empowered by Holy Spirit sent upon me from my Father to equip me and enable me! I was the Prototype of man empowered by Holy Spirit to effect the work of our Father in the earth.

And so, you must follow me, as I said, and to follow my works requires that you, as I, be *empowered* by Holy Spirit.

There is no other way. That's why I said, "without *me* you can do nothing (for the Holy Spirit is the Spirit of Jesus)." It's why I insisted that my followers wait . . . "*wait* in Jerusalem" I said to them, "until you are endued with *power from on high.*"

Power from below or from within would never do. Not for this mission! It must be from above or not at all, for yours is a battle that is not against flesh and blood (for which power from within may possibly suffice). But no, to follow me is to immediately be at war with spiritual powers against which you have no strength, unless mine!

The 'Called-out' ones

I said a moment ago that there was another 'temple' yet to come—after me. It is to that temple which I must now point you. As with each of the 'dwelling places' I have inhabited in your realm and within time, it is a sacred place, a place set aside for my presence, power, and indeed for the display of my glory!

Of course, it is none other than my Ecclesia or my 'called out ones.'[5] Yes, for I, Wisdom, as you have seen, stand at the crossroads and where the paths meet, calling people out from folly and from the broken world system and from the thrall of sin and death.

Within my Ecclesia is where I have now taken up residence among mankind. Yes, I dwell within individual hearts and of course, collectively, within the whole. Father has ordained that I, Wisdom dwell there and be, through it, displayed to the world—and how I long for it to be so! Yes, our image and likeness within

---

5. Greek ekklesia from ek, 'out from and to' and kaleo, 'to call'

the world you inhabit, in a very real sense, depends on your yielded-ness to us! Does this place limitations on us? We are able as you know, to do exceedingly above and beyond what man can imagine; however, it pleases the Father to transform you into our likeness and to have the world see us, through you!

To you this is mystery: that God should live in a flawed and sometimes even derelict house! Ah, but we are, to use one of your expressions, 'doing the house up'—it is a work in progress. Our dwelling will, in time, be seen for what it is.

Earth's wisest people

Let me assure you of this: this new house of mine is comprised of the wisest people on earth! You may be shocked that I should say this, but let me tell you why it is so.

We categorize them as the wisest because they are those who have made the wisest choice it is possible to make—the choice of light over darkness, of eternal saved-ness over lostness, of life over death! Sadly, folly can be the only description applied to those who un-choose me: if you keep refusing to choose wisdom, you have thereby chosen folly.

Yes, yes, I understand that some, perhaps many of the '*living stones*'[6] that I am using to build my house do not always act wisely—they are full of human frailty—but they have begun wisely. By taking the first step into me, they have joined themselves to Wisdom and my desire is to work with them if, and as, they learn to yield to me for I, Wisdom, have *only* and always the very best in mind for them. And, believe me, I will move heaven and earth (as only I am able) to ensure that as they learn obedience, I will cause all things—and yes, I mean *all* things to synergize for their good and blessing.[7]

---

6. See 1 Peter 2:5

7. See Romans 8:28 where Paul uses the Greek verb SUNERGEO meaning to synergise and cause to cooperate!

The Person

This is me, doing for you those things entirely beyond your scope or capability and the reason I offer this is so that you will not succumb to anxiety and the awful debilitation we know it causes.

All through your time journey *rest* has been my desire and objective for all of you. It is my offer to lift you to where I live. I do not fret; I am not overborne nor anxious for it is I who govern all things—and I invite you into what I enjoy—into the shalom of trusting my government. What was the promise of the 'Promised Land'? REST! And by that I meant productivity, fruitfulness and blessing in an environment of peace and cooperation with me. I was deliberately casting out those who had inhabited that land. They had corrupted it entirely with their gross evil which took them on a downward spiral until they were sacrificing their own offspring to their demonic imaginings! Now you know what we mean by folly. We always know when what you call civilization is beginning a death spiral because the arch-enemy of human life finds a way to trick you into killing your offspring. We see that it is occurring again in your time. Beware! It is the greatest of follies. Hasten to forsake it and embrace Wisdom and become part of the House of Wisdom we are building on earth.

When we speak of rest, we mean something bigger than what you normally understand. To most of you, rest means cessation from work and so it does to us, yet we mean much more than that. It is our desire, yes, that there be a cessation of work, but what we mean by that is your own anxiety-producing efforts to make things happen on your own. You will remember that that was the curse resulting from Adam's disobedience. Until then, all had been (as we intended) a flowing together in productive harmony. But that possibility was put out of order and was why we said, 'in worrisome toil[8] shall you eat.' That is now the fallen and out-of-order condition of your world. Yet, for those who choose wisdom—who choose to return to us, we are offering a taste of something altogether different and redeemed! For you must know that we and

---

8. In Genesis 3:17 the Hebrew word ITSTSABON is from the root ATSAB meaning to cause pain or grief.

only we have the wherewithal to govern all things, yes, even when they look hopeless, for the good of those we love!

You may say, "but do you not love all?" And the sure and unchanging answer is that we do—and that of course, is why we keep on calling—standing at every crossroads in every life with our call. But we cannot do for those who deliberately un-choose us what we determine to do for those who have changed their mind and chosen to walk with us. Those who make the wisest choice of all—and go forward day to day choosing us and trusting us—find themselves the recipients of our governance of every detail of their lives. No, we do not usurp their personhood or their individuality. We teach them how to co-function with us in a joyful 'tour-de-force' that is greater than the sum of its parts. It is life as we always intended for you. And we love it! It brings us pleasure to see our children and followers blessed and understanding what we really mean by 'rest.'

So, dear reader, it is hoped that you see just why those who have chosen partnership with us are indeed the wisest people on earth . . . and growing wiser as they trust and rest in our sovereign delight in them and our care for them. Wisdom from outside is being made available to them continually—through me![9]
Will you be among the wise? Will you trust Me?

> . . .(*Wisdom*) *cries out from the highest places of the city,*
> *"Whoever is simple, let him turn in here!"*
> *As for him who lacks understanding, she says to him,*
> *"Come, eat of my bread and drink of the wine I have mixed.*
> *Forsake foolishness and live,*
> *And go in the way of understanding."*

---

9. See 1 Corinthians 1:30 where Paul reminds us that believers are 'in' Christ Jesus 'who became *for us* wisdom from God . . .'

Afterword

BY WATCHER SHAQAAD

I HOPE YOU HAVE enjoyed travelling with me as I've tried to help you see what those are missing, who trust anything or anyone other than the Father from whom they sprang: 'The' Father who had you in mind as a unique part of his purpose even before time began.

For it is Life that they are missing. The possibility of life lived in conjunction with the One who *is* Wisdom. Life as he intended it to be lived and enjoyed! To exist without union with him is to be less than you—the 'you' of his intention and design and forethought.

To embrace him is to embrace the true 'you', for with him, and in him, is the only place where 'you' can come to life.

The reason for this is because all of the 'you-s'—that is what you call the 'we' and the 'us'—are born in alienation, having inherited alienation from Adam's line. The 'I am' image of your Creator is marred within you. It is that image that he desires to redeem and restore by having each of you 'born again' or 'born anew' into his new lineage; the new lineage he began. You can be transferred from your old 'in Adam' life to your new 'in Christ' life—if you are willing.

Afterword

His plan and provision to enable this is profound wisdom and is accomplished through the one known as Wisdom, the Logos, none other than Jesus Christ among you making a new way. It was he who provided atonement for the unbelief/sin that separated you from the Father and through whom alone, forgiveness and acceptance is offered.

The wisest thing any one of you can possibly do is to accept his offer and his accomplished work in your behalf and to begin to live in the wisdom that is from above, for you.

It is, as an ancient writer expressed it, 'above rubies.' Seek this wealth now. It is worth more than anything this transient and gone-wrong world can possibly offer. Ask him to forgive your unbelief and all the sin that accrues from that, and to enable you to believe and to receive his new life within.

Hear what Job said so long ago . . .

> "But where can wisdom be found? And where is the place of understanding?
> Man does not know its value, Nor is it found in the land of the living.
> The deep says, 'It is not in me'; And the sea says, 'It is not with me.'
> It cannot be purchased for gold, Nor can silver be weighed for its price.
> It cannot be valued in the gold of Ophir, In precious onyx or sapphire.
> Neither gold nor crystal can equal it, Nor can it be exchanged for jewelry of fine gold.
> No mention shall be made of coral or quartz, For the price of wisdom is above rubies.
> The topaz of Ethiopia cannot equal it, Nor can it be valued in pure gold.
> "From where then does wisdom come? And where is the place of understanding?
> It is hidden from the eyes of all living, And concealed from the birds of the air.
> Destruction and Death say, 'We have heard a report about it with our ears.'

Afterword

God understands its way, And He knows its place.

For He looks to the ends of the earth, And sees under the whole heavens,

To establish a weight for the wind, And apportion the waters by measure.

When He made a law for the rain, And a path for the thunderbolt,

Then He saw wisdom and declared it; He prepared it, indeed, He searched it out.

And to man He said, 'Behold, the fear of the Lord, that is wisdom, And to depart from evil is understanding.'[1]

---

1. Job 28:12–28

www.ingramcontent.com/pod-product-compliance
Lightning Source LLC
Chambersburg PA
CBHW071159090426
42736CB00012B/2388